The Growth-Minded Leader

The Growth-Minded Leader

How the Mountains You're Facing are the Path to Your Potential

Tyler Cook

ConnectEDD Publishing
Hanover, Pennsylvania

Copyright © 2025 by Tyler Cook

All rights reserved. No part of this publication may be reproduced, distributed, or transmitted in any form or by any means, including photocopying, recording, or other electronic or mechanical methods, without the prior written permission of the publisher, except in the case of brief quotations embodied in critical reviews and certain other noncommercial uses permitted by copyright law. For permission requests, contact the publisher at: info@connecteddpublishing.com

This publication is available at discount pricing when purchased in quantity for educational purposes, promotions, or fundraisers. For inquiries and details, contact the publisher at: info@connecteddpublishing.com

Published by ConnectEDD Publishing LLC
Hanover, PA
www.connecteddpublishing.com

Cover Design: Stacey Cook

The Growth-Minded Leader —1st ed. Paperback
ISBN 979-8-9988361-0-7

Praise for *The Growth-Minded Leader*

Tyler Cook has written the playbook for leaders who want to turn adversity and challenge into fuel for growth. This book will equip and inspire you to see the potential in life's obstacles. A must-read!

–Jordan Montgomery | Bestselling Author, Speaker, and Performance Coach

If you're looking for a book that will challenge you, equip you, and encourage you to take ownership of your growth, this is it. Tyler Cook takes you outside your comfort zone–a great place to navigate towards because that's where change takes place. His approach is straightforward, actionable, and exactly what you need to take your leadership to the next level.

–Damon West | Bestselling Author of *The Coffee Bean*

This book is about more than leadership–it's about transformation. Tyler Cook challenges us to lean into the hard things and pursue lasting growth in every area of our lives. *The Growth-Minded Leader* is exactly what today's leaders need.

–Clay Scroggins | Author of *How to Lead When You're Not in Charge*

The Growth-Minded Leader is one of the most transformative leadership books I've read. Tyler Cook masterfully captures the truth that you cannot lead others where you haven't gone yourself. This isn't just a book, it's a roadmap for personal and professional growth that every educator and leader needs. It's honest, practical, and deeply inspiring. If you're ready to lead with greater clarity, impact, and authenticity, this book will take you there.

–Angie Taylor | Co-Founder of Valor Global Foundation Author of *The Way of Valor*

This book is a wake-up call for every leader who knows they were made for more but feels stuck in the grind. Tyler doesn't just offer principles—he shares a pathway. His honesty, grit, and depth will challenge you to confront the things you've been avoiding and give you the tools to actually grow. If you want to lead with integrity, clarity, and purpose—start here. This is the kind of book I'll hand to the men I mentor.

–Jason Vallotton | Pastor, Author, and Founder of BraveCo

As I read through Tyler Cook's book *The Growth-Minded Leader*, I found myself constantly being challenged and encouraged at the same time. It pushed me outside my comfort zone yet reminded me of how important and life-changing the work is. Within each of us is a leader, and Tyler reminds us time and again that our true potential is only reached through intentional practices. I can't wait to re-read this book many times and share it with everyone I can. It truly left a mark on my life.

–Todd Nesloney | Director of Culture & Strategic Leadership, Speaker, Author

Tyler Cook's *The Growth-Minded Leader* is a powerful call to stop chasing titles and start leading from within. With honesty and practical tools, he shows how the hard seasons aren't obstacles—they're the very path to your potential. This book is a must-read for leaders who feel stuck, stretched thin, or ready to grow with clarity and conviction. I'd recommend it to any educator or leader who wants to climb with purpose, not just perform.

–Jessica Cabeen | Nationally Distinguished Principal, Author, Speaker

In a world full of surface-level leadership advice, Tyler Cook goes deep in *The Growth Minded Leader,* offering wisdom shaped by real life and tested in the everyday trenches of leadership and family. This isn't a book filled with theory; it's a vulnerable and powerful invitation to do the internal work that real growth requires. Tyler doesn't just write about leadership—he lives it, from the edge-of-the-bed conversations that shook him awake to the daily discipline of showing up for his family and those he leads. His honesty, humility, and practical insights make this book a gift for anyone ready to climb the mountain in front of them. If you're stuck, weary, or simply wanting more, The Growth Minded Leader will help you rise with purpose and lead from the inside out.

–Zac Bauermaster | Principal, Speaker, Author of *Leading with a Humble Heart* and *Leading with People*

Whether you're leading a team, running a business, or simply striving to become better each day, *The Growth-Minded Leader* offers an inspiring roadmap. Tyler Cook provides actionable wisdom, real-world examples, and a contagious belief that growth is always possible—even in the most challenging times!

–Matt Bresee | Business and Executive Coach

Tyler Cook doesn't just write about growth-minded leadership, he lives it. I've witnessed firsthand how Tyler leads with the same intentionality and character he calls readers to embrace in this powerful book. What makes *The Growth-Minded Leader* so compelling is that every principle he shares has been tested in the trenches of real leadership. Tyler understands that growth isn't just about professional development or hitting targets, it's about becoming the kind of person others can count on, whether that's in the classroom, the boardroom, or around the dinner table. He presents a practical roadmap forged in the real battles of leading yourself first, then others. If you're ready to stop settling for comfortable and start climbing toward your potential, this book will equip you with everything you need to take that first step ... and keep climbing.

–Derek Sanford | Lead Pastor, Grace Church, Erie, PA

The Growth Minded Leader is a powerful reminder that the mountains we face are not obstacles; they are the path. Tyler does not just write about leadership, he lives it. Through honest storytelling, the practical UNCHARTED framework, and real-world reflection questions, this book challenges readers to stop drifting and start leading every area of their life with clarity, courage, and consistency. This is a must-read for anyone serious about growth and leading with intention.

–Dr. David Arencibia | Author of *Foundations of an Elite Culture*, National Principal of the Year Finalist, Texas Principal of the Year

The Growth Minded Leader is the book every aspiring and experienced leader has been waiting for. Dr. Tyler Cook organizes his insights through the powerful UNCHARTED framework, offering a meaningful guide for leadership and for life. What makes this book truly stand out is Tyler's ability to inspire leaders to turn inward. He reminds us that beyond all the responsibilities and expectations, the most important factor in leadership success is you. With practical tools, reflection opportunities, and powerful messages woven throughout, this book encourages you to grow from within so you can lead with greater purpose and clarity.

–Dr. Brandon Beck | Teacher, Speaker, Leadership Coach

Dedication

First and foremost, to my wife, Stacey:

Your wisdom, grace, and daily pursuit of growth continue to amaze me.

Thank you for your unwavering support and unconditional love.

I love you.

To Elijah, Judah, Noah, and Anna:

I pray you would live anchored in your identity, passionate in your faith, and forever in pursuit of your potential.

The mountains are yours for the taking.

Table of Contents

Introduction 1

Chapter 1: *Leadership Starts Within* 3
    Lead Your Life. 4
    Facing the Mountain 5
    The Double Win. 6
    Stuck in the Struggle 7
    The UNCHARTED Path 8
    The Weight of Leadership. 9
    Stepping on the Trail 11
    Burn the Boats 13
    The UNCHARTED Framework 14
    Answering the Call. 16

Chapter 2: *Understanding Your Limiting Beliefs*. 17
    What is Holding You Back? 18
    Things to Quit Before You Start 19
    The Lie of Limiting Beliefs 25
    The Pike Syndrome 26
    Hidden in the Stone. 27
    Confronting the Lies 27

Rewriting the Stories that Hold You Back 29
The Science of Negativity 32
When Doubt Tries to Decide For You 33
Partnering with the Truth 34
Leadership in Action: Limiting Beliefs 37

Chapter 3: *Navigate with Vision and Purpose* 39
The Compass and the Engine 40
The Overlooked Vision 41
The Fire Inside You 42
Steadfast Through Life's Storms 43
Purpose Over "Success" 44
The Cost of Inaction 45
6 Keys to Crafting Your Vision for Growth 53
Your Legacy 54
Who You're Becoming 56
Leadership in Action: Vision and Purpose 57

Chapter 4: *Choose to Take Ownership* 57
The Shift from Excuses to Ownership 58
The Partnership for Growth 59
Self-Accountability: Your Guardrails 60
Self-Accountability in Action 62
The Cornerstone of Personal Responsibility 63
Your "Home Inspection" 64
Not More Things, But *Right* Things 65
When Ownership Creates Opportunity 66
The Value of Self-Reflection 67
It Starts with You 69
Leadership in Action: Ownership 70

TABLE OF CONTENTS

Chapter 5: *Harness Resilience* **73**
    Why Resilience Matters 74
    Don't Waste Your Hard Season 75
    Opportunities in Disguise.......................... 77
    Circling the Mountain 78
    The Stockdale Paradox 80
    Normalizing Difficulties 81
    6 Keys for Developing Resilience 83
    Built in the Battle 85
    Leadership in Action: Resilience 86

Chapter 6: *Act With Discipline and Consistency* **89**
    A Disciplined Life 90
    Discipline Over Motivation 91
    Consistency: The Name of the Game 93
    A Wake-Up Call.................................... 95
    Your Future Self Will Thank You 96
    Comfort: Your Cozy Prison 98
    The Neuroscience of Doing Hard Things.............. 99
    If a Man Works Hard, the Land Will Not Be Lazy 100
    Show Me Your Calendar, and I'll Tell You Your Priorities 102
    Boundaries.. 103
    Your Daily Habits = Your Future's Blueprint....... 104
    The Discipline Difference 106
    Leadership in Action: Discipline and Consistency .. 108

Chapter 7: *Reframe Your Mindset* **111**
    The More Pain You Expect, the More Pain You Feel.. 113
    Your Mindset ROI 114
    The Dartmouth Experiment......................... 114

Get in Your Tree Stand 116
Fixed vs. Growth Mindset. 117
Grit. 120
Smooth Seas Do Not Build Skillful Sailors 120
William Wallace 121
Trusting the Process. 122
What You Think, You Become 124
Leadership in Action: Mindset. 125

Chapter 8: *Transform Failure into Opportunities* **127**
The Lesson Under the Rock 130
Navigating Setbacks in Leadership and Life. 132
What is Your Default? 133
4 Steps to Growing Through Failure and Setbacks 134
"Good." 137
Built to Win 139
The Gift of Adversity. 140
Leadership in Action: Failure and Setbacks 141

Chapter 9: *Embrace Community and Accountability* **143**
The Cornerstone. 144
Your Support Team 145
Accountability, Support, and Feedback–The Trifecta
  for Growth 147
The Isolation Trap 148
Iron Sharpens Iron. 151
Leadership in Action: Community and Accountability 153

TABLE OF CONTENTS

Chapter 10: *Dare to Climb*..**155**
    Leave it All on the Field................................. 157
    The Power of Showing Up 158
    Choose Your Hard.. 159
    UNCHARTED... 161

Epilogue **163**
References..**165**
About the Author **171**
More from ConnectEDD Publishing **173**

Introduction

Every one of us eventually comes face to face with a humbling glimpse of who we really are, of not just what we've accomplished on the outside, but our true selves. That's exactly where I found myself not long ago.

I had the position. I had the title. As a veteran principal, author, and keynote speaker who traveled around the country developing leaders and equipping teams, I worked hard to check all the right boxes for success. Yet deep down I felt stuck, frustrated by the gap between the man I was and the one I desired to be. I knew it wasn't from a lack of ambition that I ended up there. Rather, it was a lack of understanding that true, lasting growth is a byproduct of doing the necessary work on the *inside of me*.

Inside, I lacked peace. My moments of solitude were filled with guilt, anxiety, overwhelm, and unrest. I knew something deeper needed to shift, but I didn't need more information to get there—I needed transformation. And that meant leaning into the uncomfortable process of personal growth that I had spent far too long avoiding. My wife deserved better. My kids deserved better. And those I led each day deserved better.

This process of growth wasn't one I could hustle my way over. It wasn't going to be solved by performing, stacking more accomplishments, or pretending everything was fine. It was an internal journey that required confronting my limiting beliefs, taking ownership of my life, and showing up each day in pursuit of my potential. That was the moment everything shifted. Because I realized the mountain in front of me wasn't blocking my breakthrough. It *held* my breakthrough.

This book is for the person who knows they're capable of more but feels stuck in the middle of something hard, intimidating, or even unknown. Maybe you're battling fear, burnout, or overwhelming stress. Maybe you've compromised your priorities, and your family is no longer getting the best of you. Perhaps comfort has crept in and silenced your courage. Or maybe you're doing the right things, but not seeing the kind of growth that brings lasting transformation in your life and leadership.

This book isn't about life-hacks or surface-level inspiration. It's about the deeper work—the kind that happens when you face hard things head-on, take ownership of your story, and continue climbing when everything in you wants to quit. Each chapter is a part of the mountain meant for your growth—clearing what's in the way, building resilience, choosing discipline, and developing the mindset of someone who doesn't just lead others but leads *themselves* with strength, humility, and purpose.

The Growth-Minded Leader is your call to rise. A call to stop measuring your life by titles and accolades and start building what actually matters—with character, clarity, and conviction. And it's a call to forge the path ahead, no matter what stands in front of you.

Leadership isn't about perfection. It's about showing up fully in every area of your life—in your home, your work, and your inner world. It's about becoming the kind of person who multiplies growth in others because you've done the work *in yourself*.

Those mountains you're facing? They aren't obstacles to avoid. They're the path to becoming the leader and person you were born to be.

The process won't be easy. But I promise it will be worth it.

Let's climb.

CHAPTER ONE

Leadership Starts Within

Mount Marcy is one of the legendary Adirondack High Peaks in upstate New York, located on the Great Range Traverse. Its elevation, terrain, and unpredictable weather have challenged even the most seasoned hikers. At first, the path seems inviting as adventurers set out on a gentle incline through a shaded forest. However, as the journey continues, the terrain becomes more demanding. The smooth trail gives way to steep climbs, jagged rock, and exposed drop-offs. Every step begins to feel more difficult than the last, and the higher one goes, the further away the summit feels.

As time passes, many hikers begin to question the journey. They wonder if the peak is reachable and even worth the discomfort in front of them. Soon enough, the struggle begins to chip away at even the most seasoned hikers. But, those who press on and refuse to turn back begin to realize that the hardest parts of the journey were not meant to break them but to build them. Every challenge along the way was forging inside of them the resolve and endurance necessary to continue the climb they started. And once they finally reach the summit, they discover that the greatest reward is not the breathtaking views, but who they became along the way.

The most significant obstacle for hikers was never actually the mountain itself. It was the doubt, fear, and temptation to settle for less than they were capable of. These are the very battles that prevent most people from ever attempting the climb in the first place.

Lead Your Life

The greatest challenges you face in life are not actually found in your circumstances—they are found *within yourself*. Every day, you wake up faced with a choice: you either lean into the uncomfortable process of personal growth or you settle into your comfort zone. You either confront the hard things in your life or you avoid them. You either develop your mindset or partner with your limiting beliefs.

The truth is that the life, leadership, and relationships you desire are not waiting for you in easy things. They're built in the challenges you're steering clear of, the risks you've hesitated to take, or the discipline you've exchanged for convenience.

Great leadership does not start with earning a title, leading a team, or assuming a position. Instead, leadership starts *within*. It begins the moment you take ownership of your life—when you decide to stop drifting, stop settling, and start leading every area of your life with purpose and intention.

The Growth-Minded Leader isn't about shortcuts or quick fixes. It is about confronting your limiting beliefs, reframing your mindset, developing resilience, and pursuing your potential. It's about rolling up your sleeves and applying the discipline required to become the person and leader you know you are meant to be. The greatest leaders understand their responsibility to lead themselves *first*. Not because it's *easy*, but because it's *necessary*.

So, if you have ever felt stuck—paralyzed by fear, caught in complacency, overwhelmed by distractions, or held back by your circumstances—this is your invitation to your way forward. It's time to lean into your purpose and engage in the principles required for your growth. You are worth it. Your team is worth it. Your family is worth it. Your future is worth it.

> Great leaders *lead themselves first.* Not because it's easy, but because it's necessary.

Facing the Mountain

We all face moments when we must decide whether to take ownership of our growth or stay stuck in old patterns. For many years of my own life, I avoided discomfort. I lived trapped in a cycle where the demands of my external circumstances piled on top of the unprocessed emotions that I refused to acknowledge. I had become accustomed to pushing the difficult emotions aside and avoiding confronting them at all costs. However, whenever we avoid discomfort, we reinforce the belief that we cannot handle it. Over time, this becomes a self-fulfilling prophecy—the more we run from it, the less capable we feel of overcoming it.

One night, I was sitting on the edge of my bed, completely overwhelmed by the recurring patterns and struggles I was experiencing regarding certain aspects of my relationships and career. My wife, Stacey, simply stood and listened. Then, I shook my head and uttered the same defeated phrase I used so many times before: "I don't want to think about it."

The weight of those words hung in the air. I remember the look in Stacey's eyes as she quietly responded, "Tyler, I notice you say, 'I don't want to think about it,' every time you are overwhelmed. Let me ask you: how is this working out for you?"

She was right. Her words stung deeply, but they were exactly what I needed to hear. It was a wake-up call for me. My constant avoidance of my current situation was not protecting me from discomfort; it was robbing me of the opportunity to grow through it. I was choosing to ignore what needed attention, and in doing so, I stayed buried under the mess in my mind and heart.

We become captive to whatever we are unwilling to confront. It was not until this moment of humbling clarity that I realized my avoidance only made me feel more stuck. However, my discomfort was not an enemy to avoid. It was a signal of the areas in my life that I needed to grow in maturity and discipline. One perspective sees a *threat*; the other sees an *opportunity*.

Growth and comfort rarely coexist. We must choose one or the other. When we choose to climb the mountain rather than search for a way around it, our breakthrough is often waiting for us on the path.

> We become captive to whatever we are unwilling to confront.

The Double Win

There are countless valuable books written on leadership and personal growth, many of which fill my own office shelves. Leadership books on the core principles of effective leadership, how to foster healthy cultures, and keys to building powerful teams, along with personal growth books on mindset, discipline, and purpose.

However, in my own leadership roles and working with other leaders across the country, I continue to hear the same theme repeatedly: leaders feel tired, overwhelmed, struggle to be truly present in their homes, and feel like they are on the losing end of their own personal growth journey. They feel trapped under the weight and responsibility of their leadership positions, resulting in living on "auto-pilot" in the most important areas of their lives.

These battles have created a generation of many leaders who lead well on the *outside* but lack the vision and fortitude on the *inside* to grow in the areas that ultimately matter. I wrote this book because I've also been there. While I spent years of my own life intently pursuing external goals and aspirations, I unfortunately also spent years avoiding the uncomfortable internal work of processing my emotions and disciplining my life so that I could truly win where it mattered most.

But what if I told you that you could have the *double win*? What if you could live a thriving life of peace, purpose, and internal prosperity while *also* leading your team with excellence? It is not only possible but also what you were created for—and *The Growth-Minded Leader* will help get you there.

Stuck in the Struggle

In today's world, it often feels like everyone else has it all figured out. Social media feeds are filled with filtered snapshots of success, happiness, and achievement—images of rising careers and thriving relationships. This illusion of progress and success only perpetuates the pressure to keep up, often coupled with anxiety and shame from thinking we are falling behind or not good enough. This is not only a saddening trap but also masks the deeper struggles that many of us experience. Beneath the surface are areas of our lives where we feel frustrated, hopeless, or even defeated.

In fact, research shows that while society glorifies external measures of success, internal discontentment is nearly everywhere. Workplace disengagement, relational disconnection, and a growing sense of purposelessness highlight a more revealing truth—many people lack the mindset and tools for true and lasting growth in their lives. In Gallup's

2024 "State of the Global Workplace" report, it was discovered that only 23 percent of people globally actually feel engaged and thriving in their lives, with many people desiring to grow, but struggling with the clarity and direction needed to take action (Gallup, 2024).

Additionally, the data showed a staggering 80 percent of people feel disengaged or stuck in their careers, resulting in a lack of purpose and vision for their lives. This disconnect between outward appearance and internal discontentment further underscores the reality that many people are searching for their true potential but are unsure how to reach it (Gallup, 2024).

Concerning relationships, a meta-analysis of over 165,000 participants showed that life stressors and challenges played a substantial role in the quality of their marriages and their relational growth. Of those participants, nearly half (45%) of the people surveyed also felt loneliness and disconnection in their relationships (Bühler et al., 2021).

These statistics reflect a reality that many face daily. Even further, it is an indicator that:

1. There are areas in every person's life that are not where they desire to be.
2. There is a need for a roadmap to get there.

The UNCHARTED Path

As you read this book, you may be exhausted in your leadership role, living disconnected in your marriage, or lacking discipline with your physical health. Whatever it may be, each of us has areas where we desire growth, yet we struggle to find breakthroughs time and time again. We battle discouragement, wishing for an easier path *around the mountains* that stand between where we are and the life we envision. But the reality is that your growth and potential are only found through your journey *on the mountain*.

It is forged through taking ownership of your life and confronting the lies and limiting beliefs that hold you captive.

It is developed through showing up each day with discipline, consistency, and resilience—even in the face of failure and setbacks.

It is cultivated by reframing your mindset and viewing the obstacles in front of you as an opportunity to overcome them.

And it is strengthened by inviting feedback and accountability from others into your life.

There are no shortcuts to your growth and no "easy" button. Your growth as a person, leader, spouse, and parent does not occur in the absence of difficulties and trials. It is developed through them. Only here can you develop the character and tools necessary to unlock the potential inside you.

Wherever you are as you begin reading this book, take heart. The journey of pursuing your potential is not an easy one. After all, if it were easy, everyone would do it. But you are reading this book for a reason. You know you were made for more than the reality of your current situation. So, let this be the start of your ascent toward a life of purpose and impact, starting from the *inside out*.

> Your growth does not occur in the absence of difficulties. It is developed *through* them.

The Weight of Leadership

As a leader, the demands on your life are seemingly endless. From meetings, to emails, to your position's responsibilities, your time and bandwidth are at a premium. And, as a high-capacity leader, chances are you continue to rise to the occasion despite the challenges. It's who you are and what you do, right? However, without healthy balance, proper priorities, and aligned focus, leaders are often the first to find themselves overstretched, emotionally unavailable in their homes, and treading water on the inside.

The previously mentioned Global Gallup Survey further highlights that leaders are significantly more likely to feel stress, sadness, loneliness, anger, and worry than those not in leadership roles. These internal pressures of leadership can impact more than just how you show up in the workplace. It can also affect your relationships and ultimately your well-being.

Additionally, even though many associate those in leadership roles with attributes like confidence and strength, many leaders feel like imposters beneath the surface. They feel shame as they struggle with their own growth and attempt to overcome personal challenges in their lives. Their attention and energy are focused on supporting and leading others, so they end up neglecting themselves.

In a 2023 study, the *Harvard Business Review* noted that 53 percent of leaders reported feeling burned out and exhausted due to high workloads, heavy responsibilities, and limited resources. The result? Over half the leaders interviewed admitted to compromising their own self-care and felt they had lost the capability and stamina to take on life's challenges like they once could (Klinghoffer & Kirkpatrick-Husk, 2023).

However, there is a better way. Despite the pressures and struggles that come with leadership, there is an opportunity to recalibrate your life, recharge your vision, and take the steps to truly start winning. The journey begins with taking ownership—not as a victim of your circumstances, but as the leader of your own life.

> **PAUSE AND REFLECT:**
>
> 1. *When have you found yourself struggling with the weight and pressures of leadership, resulting in overwhelm, discouragement, or burnout?*
>
> 2. *How has it impacted your personal life, relationships, and your passion to grow?*

Stepping on the Trail

No matter your season of life as you turn these pages, chances are you've had moments of wondering:

Am I living up to my full potential?

There's more in me, but why do I keep feeling stuck, circling the same challenges repeatedly?

Why can't I seem to find a lasting breakthrough in my life?

Perhaps you are feeling the lack of progress toward your goals, the ache of dissatisfaction in certain areas, or the weight of a current hardship. Yet the outcomes of your life and the growth you desire boil down to one crucial question:

What steps are you willing to consistently take to do something about it?

In the book *Atomic Habits*, James Clear states: "Every action you take is a vote for the person you wish to become" (Clear, 2018). Every day you can cast your vote. You hold the power to draw a line in the sand and move toward becoming the person and leader you have the capability to be. Let that sink in: *You are the CEO of your life.* You are not a casualty of your circumstances and are not meant to settle for less. The life and growth you seek are yours to claim—to the degree of responsibility, discipline, and unwavering commitment you are willing to embrace.

Herein lies the beauty of growth. It is not hinged on anyone else's decisions or even the *"Cards you've been dealt."* Instead, it develops *through* what you are facing. In these moments, you have the greatest opportunity to turn your obstacles into steppingstones and your adversity into your strength. That is what sets a growth-minded leader apart.

This book is not a shallow encouragement of *"If you can dream it, you can do it."* It is just the opposite. This is about taking a raw, honest inventory of your life to identify the patterns, roadblocks, and distractions holding you back and stealing from your potential. It is about conquering the mountains that keep showing up in front of you, armed with a clear vision and unshakable resolve to do the necessary courageous work. Only through this process will you find the breakthrough you've been after.

Burn the Boats

In 1519, Hernán Cortés led a Spanish expedition to Mexico to pursue wealth and conquest. When he arrived on the shores of Veracruz, he did something extraordinary and, to his men, likely terrifying–he ordered his ships to be burned. By destroying their only means of retreat, Cortés made it clear that there was no turning back. At that point, forward progress was no longer an option—it was the only way.

For his men, the burning of the ships removed the temptation of retreat to where they came from. It forced them to face their mission with steady resolve, knowing they were at the point of no return. They could no longer rely on an easy exit if things got difficult. As a result, they had to shift their mindset, focus their energy, and foster the courage to continue pressing onward. Two long years later, against incredible odds, they achieved the seemingly impossible feat of conquering the Aztec Empire (Reynolds, 1959).

> Your growth comes from taking an honest look inward, followed by deliberate actions forward.

This story of Cortés is a powerful metaphor for both your personal growth and your leadership. It represents the transformational power of deciding to stop looking back at what is comfortable or "safe" and to embrace the challenges ahead. The growth you seek requires an all-in commitment. It requires you to become uncomfortable, even when it feels scary. Therefore, it's in those moments you must ask yourself:

1. *What is the cost of staying where I am at in my life?*

2. *What could my life look like (relationships, health, goals, etc.) as a result of facing the mountain head-on and pursuing growth in those areas?*

Let the answers to these questions serve as a catalyst to help you burn the boats behind you and prepare you for the greater things ahead of you.

The UNCHARTED Framework

Any road that has yet to be traveled requires a different strategy. It requires the courage to face the unknown—fueled by the focus, discipline, and resilience necessary to endure the inevitable difficulties you will encounter along the way. The UNCHARTED Framework in this book will serve as a map to lead you toward that very potential inside you.

However, this journey is about *growth*, not *achievement*. Achievement focuses on *what I do*, but growth focuses on *who I am becoming*. This framework was created to unlock who you are *meant to be*.

Furthermore, this is not a *goal-setting* book. This is a *goal-getting* book. Setting goals is easy. Getting goals is hard. Writing things down on paper requires nothing from you, but braving the storms and pushing past your comfort takes grit. One option leaves you with a notebook full of dated entries with unfulfilled aspirations. The other refines you, builds confidence, and develops trust in yourself that you have what it takes to commit and follow through.

The Growth-Minded Leader is broken down into nine main chapters, each highlighting an integral aspect of your growth journey. Built around the acronym UNCHARTED, the framework below will serve as a tool for you to apply to your life and build momentum in the areas you need.

LEADERSHIP STARTS WITHIN

THE "UNCHARTED" FRAMEWORK
9 KEYS FOR PURSUING YOUR POTENTIAL IN LEADERSHIP AND LIFE

U	UNDERSTAND YOUR LIMITING BELIEFS
N	NAVIGATE WITH VISION AND PURPOSE
C	CHOOSE TO TAKE OWNERSHIP
H	HARNESS RESILIENCE
A	ACT WITH DISCIPLINE AND CONSISTENCY
R	REFRAME YOUR MINDSET
T	TRANSFORM FAILURE INTO OPPORTUNITIES
E	EMBRACE COMMUNITY AND ACCOUNTABILITY
D	DARE TO CLIMB

As we progress through these principles, the UNCHARTED Framework will guide you in navigating the common challenges of growth and leadership. This framework's value lies in its ability to simplify your growth journey into actionable steps, making it attainable and sustainable, regardless of your starting point.

However, as you integrate these principles into your life, understand there will be resistance. Old mindsets have a way of trying to dig their heels in. Old habits will subtly try to talk you into familiar routines. Not to mention, fear does not give up easily. When this happens, it is not a sign of *failure*—it is a sign of *progress*. Every victory, no matter how small, is a step toward building a life you know is waiting for you on the other side of whatever mountain you may be facing.

Answering the Call

The Growth-Minded Leader is a call to your fullest potential—the kind of potential that does not settle for less than you know, deep down, that you were created for. However, to truly move the needle in that direction—fullness and connection in your relationships, clarity of your mind, peace in your emotional health, and effectiveness in your leadership, you will be required to *do the work*.

If you feel out of alignment with your ultimate vision, the weight of unfulfilled goals, or the nagging doubt of, *but what if…*, know that this moment is not unique to you. It is universal. But the difference lies in how you respond. Most people choose to sidestep it by retreating into familiar routines, waiting for "the right time," or surrendering to the overwhelm that leaves them paralyzed.

But *what if* you stopped waiting? *What if* you leaned in, embraced the hard, and passionately pursued what is available for you in your life? It is time to make that shift. Don't focus on perfection or immediate transformation; instead, focus on building your mindset and following through with action that leads to daily progress. As you stand at the foot of the mountain, ask yourself this honest question:

How much longer am I going to avoid who I am capable of becoming, in order to continue with what I am comfortable doing?

Let this question engage you in the gutsy face-off with the difficult things you've been avoiding. Remember, growth does not occur in the easy moments. It's instead forged in the ones that *challenge you*. As you move through these pages, I invite you to take that first step—not simply toward external success, but toward a *better version of yourself*. The path ahead will stretch you, but it will also shape you. Let's start the climb.

CHAPTER TWO

Understand Your Limiting Beliefs

THE "UNCHARTED" FRAMEWORK
9 KEYS FOR PURSUING YOUR POTENTIAL IN LEADERSHIP AND LIFE

U	UNDERSTAND YOUR LIMITING BELIEFS
N	NAVIGATE WITH VISION AND PURPOSE
C	CHOOSE TO TAKE OWNERSHIP
H	HARNESS RESILIENCE
A	ACT WITH DISCIPLINE AND CONSISTENCY
R	REFRAME YOUR MINDSET
T	TRANSFORM FAILURE INTO OPPORTUNITIES
E	EMBRACE COMMUNITY AND ACCOUNTABILITY
D	DARE TO CLIMB

The traveler couldn't help but stop and stare. A group of mighty elephants stood quietly in the middle of a circus camp in a bustling village in India. Their massive forms were tethered by a simple restraint of a thin rope tied around one leg. No chains or anchors, just a piece of fraying cord. These massive animals could snap the rope with minimal effort, yet they simply stood still.

For a moment, the traveler thought it was a trick. Surely, these powerful creatures could easily escape. Yet, they didn't even try. Curious, the traveler approached a trainer nearby and asked,

"How do these ropes hold them? Why don't the elephants try to break free?"

The trainer smiled. "When they are young, we tie them with this same rope. At that age, it is strong enough to hold them. They try to pull and break free, but they learn early on that they cannot escape. As they grow older, they carry that belief with them. Even now as adults, they never attempt to escape because they don't believe they can."

At that moment, the traveler was struck with a startling realization. The elephants were not held back by the rope, but rather by their own minds (*Hutchinson, 2019*).

What Is Holding You Back?

What is your rope? What is the story you've been telling yourself that may seem like the truth, but is actually stealing from your life? Most of us are like the elephants—tethered to belief systems, fears, or thought patterns that cast a shadow in our minds and hold us back from what we are capable of.

Perhaps it's a failure or pain you've experienced in the past that you have vowed not to experience again. Maybe it was a crippling statement that someone spoke to you years ago that has replayed over and over in your mind. Or, it could be the pressure you put on yourself to perform,

UNDERSTAND YOUR LIMITING BELIEFS

provide, and please others that drives you, but ultimately leaves you feeling defeated.

These "ropes" often hide beneath the surface yet sit in the driver's seat of our minds. The narratives might feel real, but they are as flimsy as that piece of fraying rope. The good news, however, is that, unlike the elephants, we can examine and change these belief systems by recognizing the stories that hold us back.

Confronting those lies and mindsets might feel like they oppose your present reality because they are just that—lies masquerading as truth. However, to confront those things in your life, you must first see the rope for what it really is—not a barrier, but a *belief*.

As we move through this chapter, we will explore how to identify the mental "ropes" that often hinder us. Additionally, you will learn how to challenge and ultimately break free from the limiting beliefs, fears, and habits that obstruct your growth. For your growth isn't solely dependent on what you are pursuing, but also what you are holding onto.

> Your growth isn't solely dependent on what you are pursuing, but also what you are holding onto.

Things to Quit Before You Start

There are mountains for you to conquer in your life—areas that may have seemed insurmountable, which have caused you to feel powerless, hopeless, and discouraged. Perhaps, it is not because you don't have the *right* things in your proverbial "backpack" that we all carry in life, but because you have the *wrong* things weighing you down.

If you want to progress in your growth, there are some things that you need to *quit* first, such as certain mindsets, beliefs, and unhealthy patterns of thinking. Consider the seven thought patterns below.

Which of these are unnecessary weights in your backpack? Take time to foster self-awareness, identify the unhealthy thought patterns, and start reframing your thinking.

1. **Quit Complaining**

If it's within your control, you are responsible for taking action. If it's outside your control, you are wasting your energy thinking about it.

What are the things that are in your control?
Your words, actions, behaviors, effort, and choices.
What are the things outside of your control?
Other people's words, actions, behaviors, choices, emotions, and mistakes.

Neuroscience research has conducted several studies on the detrimental effects of complaining. Throughout your brain exists a collection of synapses. Whenever you have a negative thought and complain, an electrical charge is triggered, allowing those synapses to grow closer (Hayden, 2024). This, in turn, makes it easier for your brain to have those same thoughts again. Your brain literally rewires its own circuitry based on your positive or negative thoughts. So, next time you find yourself complaining, remind yourself: *I am literally rewiring my brain for doom and gloom.* Yikes.

2. **Quit Worrying About Other People's Opinions**

Two traps we often find ourselves falling into are:

1. Worrying about what other people think about us.
2. Believing that other people think about us in the first place.

The "Spotlight Effect" is a common psychological bias where we overestimate how much other people are paying attention to our actions, behaviors, appearance, or results. Most people are too focused on their own lives to notice us as much as we think they do (Heflick, 2011). When we pay too much attention to what we perceive other people think about us, we take our eyes off our goals and compromise our authenticity. We toe the line of falling into the trap of people-pleasing, which is a perilous journey that never leads anywhere. Instead, it just keeps us focused on the opinions of others. It is a bottomless pit.

3. **Quit Focusing on Perfection**
Perfection is a myth. It is a thief that robs you of the joy of progress, keeping you caught in discontentment. Focusing on perfection may seem noble and even logical as a high performer, but the fallacy of "perfect" is a subtle enemy to your growth. You may think to yourself:

I have high standards for myself, and nothing is wrong with that.

You are right—to an extent. While having a standard of excellence is certainly honorable, there is a fine line between living driven and principled in this way, and the immense pressure and burden it can put on you that blinds you from the progress you are actually making. One is a catalyst, and the other holds you captive.

There is no such thing as "perfect" in life—no relationship, no career, and no decision. Therefore, when the inevitable struggles arise, the pressure for perfection mounts. True growth, however, occurs in the hard, messy, and challenging moments of your life. Instead of the mythical idea of perfection, focus on your *direction*:

Are you moving forward?
Are you faithfully stewarding what you have?
Are you reflective and teachable?
Are you living with the discipline and resolve to keep improving each day?

If you can answer yes to those questions, give yourself the grace to enjoy the process. *Progress* will sustain you, but *perfection* will inevitably drain you.

4. Quit Comparing Yourself to Others

There will always be someone who has more than you. There will always be someone better than you. And there will always be someone who appears to be a step ahead of you. However, what you don't see is the price they paid to get there—the sacrifices they have made, the hardships and trials they have endured, and the battles they have fought and won are often unseen by others.

Picture yourself driving down a four-lane interstate. Imagine seeing cars next to you on either side, driven by others who are also on a journey. Now, imagine taking your eyes off your lane and trying to drive down the road by looking only at those other cars. This will inevitably lead to disaster.

Why? Because the more you compare yourself to others, the more you take your eyes off your own lane. If your growth is not hinged on the progress of others, then your time, attention, and energy are not best spent focusing on their lives. Besides, the illusion of others' lives and successes on the surface are not always what they seem.

If you find yourself slipping into jealousy, discouragement, or hopelessness when you see the progress of those around you, it is time to reframe your perspective. Celebrate their wins. Ask yourself, *What can I learn from them?* Perhaps there is wisdom from their journey that can benefit yours. Keep your eyes fixed on your lane. And remember that comparison is the thief of joy.

5. Quit Blaming Other People and Other Things for Your Circumstances

Do you constantly feel like you have no control over your situation? Like the cards are simply stacked against you and there is nothing you can do about it? Like life is just *unfair*? If you find yourself blaming other people or things for your life's circumstances or problems, you may be struggling with a *victim mentality*. This perspective is a breeding ground for resentment and passivity because we feel like

UNDERSTAND YOUR LIMITING BELIEFS

other factors are more powerful in dictating our future than we are. This will be discussed in more detail later, but honestly assessing our tendencies and acknowledging our unhealthy perspectives is key. Remember, you can be a powerful person who is in control of your response to life.

6. Quit Overthinking

Most overthinking comes from the belief that it is the *decision* that ultimately matters. However, it is the *action* and follow-through that ultimately determine the success of your decision (Bloom, 2024).

There are so many people who are capable of growing and building the life that they want. However, far fewer actually execute. You may have heard the term "Analysis paralysis." This is the paralyzing feeling that stems from the fear of making the wrong decision, which ultimately leads to no decision at all.

Of course, preparation, planning, and analyzing is necessary. But beware of the pitfalls of over planning. Your ability to act, adapt, and follow through amidst difficulties or unknowns is where meaningful progress happens. Overthinking, however, will steal your peace and keep you spinning your tires until the tread is gone.

7. Quit Your Distractions

Endless distractions are fighting for your attention, such as social media, television, food, novelty, or simply the busyness of life. These distractions are often in direct opposition to your growth and to attaining your goals. It could be doom scrolling on your phone, the next episode of your Netflix binge, or the comfort food in your pantry. Or, the seemingly insignificant things subtly keeping you preoccupied just enough for you to feel "busy" but never productive.

Our brains are wired for the shiny things—the dopamine bursts. They feel good in the moment but are often empty and unfulfilling in the long term. However, building anything meaningful and lasting in life is done by showing up in the boring basics—the daily discipline, execution, and consistency.

What is the first step? It's becoming aware of what is distracting you. Ask yourself the question:

If I continue spending time on this, will it move me closer to or further away from my vision and goals?

This is the true test.

PAUSE AND REFLECT:

1. *Which of these seven thought patterns/perspectives resonate with you the most?*

2. *Where did this thought pattern originate from?*

3. *What steps can you take to confront this area of your life and reframe your perspective?*

UNDERSTAND YOUR LIMITING BELIEFS

The Lie of Limiting Beliefs

Sometimes, the most familiar things in life sabotage us without us even being aware of them. Fear. Doubts. Habits. Mindsets. That is why we must be diligent in taking regular inventory of our lives to determine what thoughts and belief systems are bringing life to us and which ones are stealing from us, such as the following:

I'm not good enough.
I don't have the time to pursue my goals.
I'll never have a marriage like I dreamed of.
I'll never find a job that I truly love.
It's too much of an uphill battle to get fit and healthy.
My work doesn't measure up to that of my colleagues.
I am just not a lucky person.
I've already missed my chance.
If I ask for help or admit my struggle, people will judge me.
I just can't seem to catch a break.
I'll always stay stuck in this situation.

The list goes on. For most of us, there is no shortage of limiting beliefs that filter through our minds each day. Some are conscious, some are subconscious, but they all have an impact. Some of the unfortunate costs of limiting beliefs in our lives are things like not taking risks, not pursuing new opportunities, sidestepping difficult conversations, avoiding vulnerability in relationships, and countless others. At the core, limiting beliefs are beliefs about yourself or your situation that *restrict* you in some way. They are often false accusations that you make about yourself or your perceived circumstances in life.

Your self-limiting beliefs deceive and hinder you because these thoughts and perceptions prevent you from doing something you are *indeed quite capable of doing* (even though you may not think you are).

They can derive from many factors, but they generally all stem from the same place: our brain's desire to protect us from pain in the future. However, the very place your limiting beliefs may be protecting you from is the *very territory you need to conquer* for the sake of your growth and potential (Kristensen, 2014).

The Pike Syndrome

In 1873, German Zoologist Dr. Karl Mobius conducted an experiment in which he placed a large pike fish into a glass tank with smaller bait fish, which the predator soon devoured. (Clemmer, 2014) Then, Mobius inserted a clear glass divider in the middle of the tank, separating the pike from a new supply of small fish. As the pike pursued its next meal, it painfully continued hitting its snout on the invisible barrier, unable to accomplish what it intended.

After a time, the pike no longer went after its prey. The fish resigned itself to the fact that it was unable to catch its meal, circling its own side of the tank instead and avoiding the glass barrier altogether.

Mobius then carefully removed the glass barrier. To his surprise, the pike continued to circle its own side of the tank but never crossed the line where the divider once was. Even as the bait fish cautiously swam over to the pike's side of the tank, the predator refused to eat them. Later in the experiment, the pike eventually laid at the bottom of the tank and died of exhaustion and starvation, even though an abundance of food surrounded it (Clemmer, 2014).

For many of us, there are situations in our lives where we are not much different than the pike. We are limited by the perceived barriers that prevent us from moving forward and pursuing challenges. Or we may have felt the sting of failure, believing that we do not have what it takes to succeed. While these feelings may be subconscious, our fears, past experiences, and self-doubt can result in us avoiding the pursuit of the very potential available to us.

Hidden in the Stone

In 1464, the Cathedral Works Committee of Florence, Italy, had an 18-by-8-foot marble block extracted from the renowned Carrara quarry in Tuscany, Italy, to bring to life their vision of a statue that would stand in the city. However, upon its arrival, renowned sculptors examined the marble block and deemed it flawed and "useless" due to visible cracks and defects. As a result, the stone was left untouched for forty years because no one believed it was worth sculpting.

However, in 1501, Michelangelo saw potential where others only saw flaws. Entrusted with the commission, he began to carve, transforming the discarded stone over the next three years into one of the most celebrated sculptures in history—David. When asked about his process of creating the famous statue, he stated, "I saw the angel in the marble and carved until I set him free" (Vasari, 1991).

Limiting beliefs often work similarly in our lives. Many of us go through life feeling like we are always lacking something–talent, opportunities, intelligence, or even a better upbringing. We tell ourselves we are not smart enough, strong enough, or capable enough. As a result, we stay "trapped in the marble," unable to realize our full potential. The truth is, everything we need is already inside us. The problem is not a lack of potential but the layers of doubt, fear, and limiting beliefs that keep it buried. These perceived shortcomings will continue to hold us back unless we are intentional to chip away with courage, truth, and consistency–just as Michelangelo did with the marble.

Confronting the Lies

Throughout my life, I prided myself on pursuing goals and achievements. I always had a target on the horizon that I aimed at, and I relentlessly pursued it until it was obtained. It felt noble–like I was being faithful with my abilities and the opportunities in front of me.

However, it never felt like it was enough. Even after accomplishing something or reaching a personal goal, I would feel discontented and even like I was failing if I was not immediately running after the next thing. I lacked peace even in my success, which was a red flag and indicator there was more going on beneath the surface.

It was not until I began to look inward and get curious that I realized that much of my self-worth was found in my accomplishments. Deep down, I felt that if I accomplished great things, I would be great. If I achieved something significant or valuable, it would mean I was significant and valuable, also.

I began to lean in and look for the lies and limiting beliefs that were holding me captive. As I began the vulnerable process of self-reflection, I started remembering times as a child when I would pack my bag to visit my biological father on the weekends. I would feverishly look around my bedroom for things to show him to impress him. It could be a trophy, a good grade on a paper, or even a story of something noteworthy I did that would make him proud. Unknowingly, I began to associate my own value with what I had accomplished and believed the lie that my worth hinged on *what I did*, rather than *who I was*.

Without realizing it, these subtle thought patterns and lies as a boy continued to steal from my life into my adult years. If I was not in pursuit of something to accomplish, I felt like the "meter" of my own worth began to drop. Nothing ever felt like enough. It stole from my peace, being present in my home, and truly appreciating the milestones and growth occurring in my life.

It wasn't until I developed the self-awareness to recognize these lies and limiting beliefs—and confronted them with truth and tenacity—that I began to understand that my worth is found in *who I am*, not simply in *what I do*.

But knowing the truth and living it out are two different things. Breaking free from years of false belief required intentional work. I had to consciously examine the thoughts that surfaced when I *wasn't* chasing the next goal. I started asking myself hard, but necessary, questions:

Why do I feel restless when I'm not achieving?
What do I believe about my worth when the work stops?
And most importantly—*what is actually true about me?*

I committed to replacing lies with truth, reminding myself that my value wasn't something I had to earn. I set boundaries with my time, giving myself permission to celebrate progress rather than immediately moving on to the next challenge. I learned to pause—to acknowledge growth instead of only measuring success by accomplishments. And I surrounded myself with people who saw my worth beyond my work— those who reminded me, when I forgot, that I was already enough.

Over time, a shift took place. It wasn't instant, and even now, I must stay aware to resist slipping back into "performance mode." But the pressure to prove myself—the lies that once dictated my worth—no longer have the same influence in my life. And it all started with the courage to draw a line in the sand, confront the lies, and renew my mind to the truth of where my value comes from.

Rewriting the Stories that Hold You Back

Below are 3 steps to overcome your limiting beliefs. This process requires both self-awareness and humility because many beliefs can camouflage as wisdom. Additionally, it may even feel embarrassing to admit them. But the process is worth it because the cost of believing them is more expensive than you may realize.

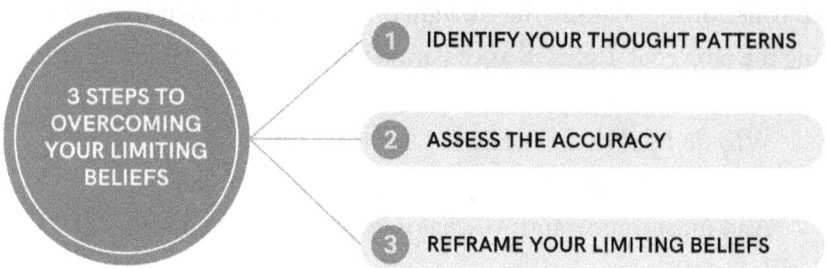

1. Identify Your Thought Patterns

These beliefs often present themselves as a thought in your head rather than something you say out loud. Pay attention to your recurring negative thoughts, examine your self-talk, and identify patterns of avoidance or feeling "stuck." By looking for those thoughts (red flags) that show up repeatedly and writing them out on paper, you can better separate fact from fiction to determine their validity, versus the story you are telling yourself.

Examples:
"I feel _____ when…"
"When _____ happens, my next thought usually is…"
"I often find myself thinking negatively about _____."

2. Assess the Accuracy

Become a scientist and get to the bottom of your beliefs. When a negative belief presents itself, take a moment to pause and analyze it. Look for evidence to determine if it is true or coming from fear, shame, or unprocessed pain. *Cognitive Behavior Therapy* is a common, evidence-based practice used by psychologists, involving a technique called *Socratic Questioning*. It utilizes a series of focused, open-ended questions that encourage you to reflect on your thoughts (Celestine, 2015). This allows you to challenge your thinking and ensure your thoughts are based on sound logic before allowing them to dictate your emotions and behaviors.

Examples:
What is the evidence for this thought?
Could I be making any assumptions here?
Is this thought based on an emotional reaction or the evidence in front of me?

3. **Reframe Your Limiting Beliefs**

After identifying and assessing your limiting beliefs, rephrase them into something empowering and positive that drives you toward who you desire to be. Although this may seem like an intuitive next step, this approach can feel forced and even like you are lying to yourself if your limiting belief has a significant foothold in your life. If that is the case, below is an example that allows you to give grace to yourself during the process:

You may experience intense feelings of anxiety when it comes to having difficult, yet necessary, conversations in your life, for fear of damaging your relationships or offending others. As a result, you don't speak up and often find yourself compromising against your better judgment. Rather than reframing your beliefs by saying to yourself:

> *I have hard conversations and don't feel scared about it. I am not worried about the impact on my relationships.*
> (This is not realistic at the moment and will have minimal benefit for you in building trust with yourself as you reframe your sabotaging thought patterns.)
> Instead, try something like:
> *I am a man (or woman) who is becoming more confident in my ability to have uncomfortable conversations in my life. Because I truly care about the relationships in my life, I am willing to be courageous, share my feelings, and allow myself to be known and heard.*

Can you feel the difference? The first is trying to *convince* yourself you are something you are currently not. The other affirms the fact that you are *growing, progressing, and intentionally developing* a new mindset when approaching something hard or scary. Reframing your thoughts is about the process of who you are *becoming*, because your growth is more than an arrival point. It is about the daily journey you are on for the rest of your life. Below are some other examples of ways to reframe your thinking:

I'm stuck. → *Breakthrough is in my control.*
It's too late. → *Now is the perfect time to start.*
I'm not ready. → *I will learn and grow as I go.*
This is too hard. → *This will make me stronger.*
I don't have time. → *I will make time for this.*
I am not good enough. → *I have what it takes to grow and improve.*
I don't have the resources. → *I will be faithful with what I do have.*

The Science of Negativity

It is astounding how quickly we default to negative thinking in life. It is a slippery slope that can be hard to resist. Even scarier is that a simple "snowflake" of negativity can quickly become an "avalanche" in our minds before we even realize it. Research has shown that the average person has approximately 6,000 thoughts per day, 85 percent of which are negative in nature. Even further, 95 percent of those thoughts are repeating themselves day after day (Leahy, 2005). This is how our brains are constructed. Our Amygdala and Limbic System are built to notice threats to protect our survival. In ancient times, it was used to protect us from danger like a predator. Today, the same parts of our brains are more cognitive in function–involving things like our finances, whether we are loved, or if we are succeeding in work and life.

When we perceive threats of difficulty, challenge, or emotional risk, it activates our *Amygdala*–the alarm bell of our brains. This almond-shaped region uses two-thirds of its neurons to look for bad news, meaning it is *primed to go negative*. These perceived negative experiences then get immediately stored in our memory, as opposed to positive experiences, which need processed for a longer period before transitioning to long-term storage (Hanson, 2010).

What's the bottom line? Fostering self-awareness is vital to understanding your tendency to focus on the negative and avoid the challenging things in your life. Your brain seeks comfort, but your growth occurs in the difficult things you are actually hardwired to avoid.

> Your brain seeks comfort, but your growth occurs in the difficult things you are actually hardwired to avoid.

When Doubt Tries to Decide for You

Our limiting beliefs subtly try to talk us out of our potential. They operate in the background–shaping how we see ourselves, what we believe we are capable of, and even what we are willing to attempt.

Dr. Ellen Ochoa, the first Hispanic woman to explore space, nearly disqualified herself from her potential–not because she lacked the *skills*, but because she questioned whether she even *belonged*. Early in Ochoa's career, she doubted she was "NASA material." She questioned if she fit the mold of what NASA was looking for and nearly talked herself out of applying. That is the deceptive power of limiting beliefs. They not only affect how we think–they also shape what we do. Or, in many cases, what we don't do.

Fortunately, with the guidance of mentors in Ochoa's life, she began to recognize the impact of her self-doubt. Rather than giving in to her inner critic, she committed to reframing her thinking, gaining experience, and focusing on what she could control. After NASA finally selected her for the astronaut program, she realized how close she had been to letting fear steal her opportunity. The only thing that ever really stood between her and that moment was her *belief in herself*. On April 8, 1993, Ochoa made history as the first Hispanic woman in space aboard the Space Shuttle Discovery. Later in her career, she became the Director of NASA's Johnson Space Center—the same institution where she once questioned whether she belonged (Ochoa, E., n.d.).

Talent and intelligence are not the ultimate predictors of our growth. Instead, most of our success hinges on our mindset and willingness to face the loudest voices of opposition, which usually come from *within*. Ochoa did not become an astronaut because she was fearless. She became one because she refused to let fear decide for her.

This struggle, known as "imposter syndrome," plagues far too many leaders. These feelings of inadequacy cut to the core of our identity, impact our confidence, and make us question whether we truly belong in the positions we hold or pursue. Growth-minded leaders are not without feelings of doubt–they refuse to partner with it. In other words, the requirement of your growth does not solely depend on the *measure of your confidence*; it is built on your courage to *take the steps forward, regardless.*

Partnering with the Truth

Your beliefs shape your reality. The narratives you choose to partner with will either propel you forward or hold you back from what you are meant for. The moment you take ownership of your life and thoughts by challenging those beliefs, you begin to clear the path to your potential.

That is why it's so important to be self-aware and renew your mind daily to the truth of who you are becoming, even if it feels "forced" at first. Because when you do it consistently, you actually "rewire" your brain and neural pathways to help the truth "stick."

UNDERSTAND YOUR LIMITING BELIEFS

It doesn't mean the negative thoughts disappear, but it means you are developing the fortitude to choose a different perspective. Remember, you are what you think. So, choose your diet wisely. From there, the next question becomes: What are you actually moving *toward* in your life?

Your growth is not just about leaving the old thought patterns behind. It is also about embracing a vision that pulls you towards your purpose. Without clarity on where you are going, you will lack the direction and strategy to get there. In the next chapter, we will uncover the power of *vision and purpose*, which will serve as the compass and fuel to guide you toward the life and leadership you are capable of achieving.

LEADERSHIP IN ACTION: LIMITING BELIEFS

Your limiting beliefs not only impact your personal growth but also influence your effectiveness as a leader and the culture you create among your team. These beliefs shape how you make decisions, handle challenges, and engage with people.

For instance, you might believe, *If I delegate this task, it won't be done correctly,* or *I have to do everything myself for it to be done right.* This belief can prevent you from empowering your team, keeping you stuck in a cycle of micromanagement and overwhelming responsibility. Over time, it creates an overburdened leader and an underdeveloped team. Instead, trust in the unique strengths of those you lead and communicate that trust with sincerity. When you release authority and empower others, you foster a culture of autonomy and growth.

Another limiting belief many leaders face is the pressure to be experts in everything. I remember my first year as a principal, sitting in meetings with teachers who were masters in their craft. Their knowledge, experience, and passion were inspiring, but I felt the constant pressure to prove myself to them. I would ask myself, *How can I lead effectively if I don't have the answers?* This belief created unnecessary stress and hindered my ability to tap into the collective strength of our team. However, over time, I learned that effective leadership does not solely hinge on having all the answers—it involves creating space for collaboration, listening to others, and learning from them. Humility in leadership does not signify weakness; it signifies authenticity and a willingness to grow alongside your team.

Finally, imposter syndrome, as mentioned in Ochoa's story above, is an all-too-prevalent limiting belief facing many leaders.

This inner voice whispers, *I'm not qualified for this*, or *At some point, people will realize I'm not as good as they think*. These thoughts, if left unconfronted, will erode your confidence, increase your anxiety, and ultimately hinder your ability to lead at your full potential. The truth is that every leader experiences moments of self-doubt. The key is to challenge these beliefs head-on and reframe them with the truth that you are even more capable than you realize.

As a leader, it is also essential to recognize that those you lead also struggle with limiting beliefs. Whether doubts about their abilities, fear of failure, or insecurities about their place on the team, these beliefs can negatively impact their performance and growth. Your role as a leader is not only to identify your own limiting beliefs but also to model how to overcome them and create opportunities for others to do the same.

Your Pursuit of Growth:

1. Challenge your inner narrative, specifically regarding your leadership role. Identify any beliefs about your leadership limiting you or replaying a message contrary to your growth and success. Assess the accuracy of your beliefs and determine if they are rooted in fear or fact.
2. Model growth for your team. You are not the only one who struggles with limiting beliefs. As you begin to recognize and overcome these areas that are hindering you, share examples with your team and provide opportunities for their own reflection and growth, such as, "What's a belief you have about your abilities that might be holding you back?" Be a catalyst for developing people from the inside out.

CHAPTER THREE

Navigate with Vision and Purpose

THE "UNCHARTED" FRAMEWORK
9 KEYS FOR PURSUING YOUR POTENTIAL IN LEADERSHIP AND LIFE

U	UNDERSTAND YOUR LIMITING BELIEFS
N	NAVIGATE WITH VISION AND PURPOSE
C	CHOOSE TO TAKE OWNERSHIP
H	HARNESS RESILIENCE
A	ACT WITH DISCIPLINE AND CONSISTENCY
R	REFRAME YOUR MINDSET
T	TRANSFORM FAILURE INTO OPPORTUNITIES
E	EMBRACE COMMUNITY AND ACCOUNTABILITY
D	DARE TO CLIMB

In 2005, Jessica Jackley was a young woman with a desire to confront the challenges of poverty in underdeveloped countries. She not only burned with passion to do something meaningful with her life that would help others in need, but she knew she needed to develop the capacity within her to turn her vision into a reality (Jackley, 2015).

Jessica envisioned a process for people to make small loans to entrepreneurs in impoverished areas, enabling them to start their own businesses. This idea was more than simply offering charity. It was about changing people's lives by empowering and enabling them to create lasting change for both their families *and* communities.

However, like most visions, the end result was more glamorous than the process of getting there. Jessica faced skepticism and doubt from potential partners. Many questioned whether it would work, and she often found herself battling her limiting beliefs and fear of failure. She was not an expert in finance or international development. She did not have all the answers, and at times, the challenge felt insurmountable.

However, Jessica never lost sight of her vision of dedicating her life to making an impact on the lives of others. That very fire inside her gave her the clarity, resilience, and perseverance to push through the inevitable obstacles that arose along the way. As a result, *Kiva* was founded.

Fast forward to today, Kiva's global impact has been nothing short of amazing. As of 2024, Kiva has funded 2.3 million micro-loans to people worldwide in countries on every major continent, totaling over $5 billion and reaching over five million people across the globe (Kiva's Impact, n.d.).

This is the power of vision. You do not need to have everything figured out, but you do need to take the first step. And that first step could impact more people than you ever imagined.

The Compass and the Engine

Vision and purpose serve as both a compass and an engine for your growth. Both are essential yet play different roles in your journey.

Your vision is your *compass*, which guides you toward the person you aspire to become and the potential inside you. It provides clarity and direction, helping ensure you stay aligned with your goals when life gets noisy or distractions creep in. A strong vision for your life enables you to recalibrate when you find yourself drifting off course, whether from life's circumstances or simply settling into your comfort zone. The more you stay focused on your vision, the more it dials in your pursuit of growth. It helps you recognize when you've strayed off course and realigns you to what matters most. Additionally, a strong vision prevents you from giving in to distractions or compromise. Your compass is not just there for when you are lost. It helps ensure you never get lost in the first place.

Purpose, on the other hand, is the *engine* that drives your growth forward. It keeps you disciplined and on track even when the path gets tough. However, one of these without the other can lead to an imbalance in your life.

Direction without drive leads to stagnation, while drive without direction can lead to unproductive busyness. Together though, vision and purpose form a powerful partnership. Vision ensures you are growing in the right direction, while purpose provides the fuel to keep going. When you engage with your vision and purpose on a daily basis, you build a life of intentional growth that influences not only yourself but everyone you lead.

> Your vision ensures you are growing in the right direction. Your purpose provides the fuel to keep going.

The Overlooked Vision

As a leader, pouring your energy and focus into crafting a vision for your team or organization is natural. Creating a vision that inspires others and illuminates a clear path forward is one of the intangible qualities of great leaders. However, when it comes to our own personal growth, this kind of intentionality and commitment can become neglected without necessarily realizing it.

This is because our personal growth requires a different level of vulnerability and intention that is far less shiny. It does not come with external validation and is only built behind the scenes. Furthermore, as leaders, we tend to give so much of our energy to supporting and growing others that we tend to overlook our own growth as a byproduct. As the old saying goes, "A carpenter's house is never finished." For too many leaders, the "house" that is neglected is on the inside.

This chapter invites you to step back and ask the question: *What is your vision for your own growth, health, relationships, and legacy?*

> Growth-minded leaders don't just shape the world around them. They are also deliberate about transforming the world *inside of them.*

Growth-minded leaders don't just shape the world around them. They are also deliberate about transforming the world *inside of them.* When this happens, they are more impactful in *every* area of their life, because leadership ultimately starts *within*.

The Fire Inside You

What is the fire that burns inside you? What growth areas do you long to see progress in your life? These could be the dreams that surface during quiet moments—those personal conversations you replay in your mind or the aspirations you share with your closest friends. What type of person do you want to become? What kind of legacy do you want to leave among others?

Some of you may already feel aligned with your purpose and are refining your vision for getting there by trimming away the things that do not add value to your life. On the other hand, you may know where you want to go but feel hindered by circumstances or mindsets that have kept you from progressing in the ways you desire. Yet for others, you may feel at a standstill altogether—even though you know you have more potential than your current life reflects.

Wherever you are, take heart. Let your discontentment be the very spark that ignites change in your life. When you are willing to turn your dissatisfaction into *action*, it becomes an *opportunity*. Remember, growth is a daily choice and results from you braving against any resistance standing between where you are and where you are going.

Steadfast Through Life's Storms

When Nelson Mandela was imprisoned in South Africa for twenty-seven years for standing up for the freedom of his country's citizens, he faced unthinkable adversity. The toll of nearly three decades of physical labor in a lime quarry, limited communication with his wife and daughters, and the psychological hardship of prolonged isolation in a cell without a bed or plumbing was something most could not imagine. Yet, even amid his circumstances, Mandela never lost sight of his vision of a free and democratic South Africa where all citizens, regardless of race, could live with the same liberties as their neighbors (Mandela, 2014).

Instead of succumbing to despair, Mandela used his time in prison to develop himself. He sharpened his leadership skills, deepened his education, and strengthened his mindset for the long journey ahead.

His unwavering purpose to a free and united South Africa was the engine that drove him to keep going, despite his daunting reality.

When Mandela was offered his release in exchange for compromising his vision, he refused. Even though it would have meant personal freedom, Mandela stated that true freedom would only come when the oppressive regime was dismantled. It was his ability to hold fast to his vision and purpose that sustained him, and the character he developed through his trials that gave him the strength to endure.

Years later, after his release from prison, Mandela became the president of South Africa and guided his country through a peaceful transition to democracy. Instead of seeking revenge, he became a voice for reconciliation, displaying the strength and wisdom needed to unite his nation.

In your life, there will be hardships, temptations to take the easier route, scenarios to compromise your values, or times you will feel like giving up hope. But, when you allow your vision to guide your steps and your purpose to sustain you, you can grow through life's fiercest storms and emerge stronger as a result.

Purpose Over "Success"

Success, as the world typically defines it, is a moving target, often measured in titles, accomplishments, and accolades. Yet, many times this leaves people feeling empty and unfulfilled. Purpose, however, is deeply rooted in conviction and meaning. When we become solely driven by the pursuit of *success*, we risk chasing external validation rather than prioritizing what actually matters most to us. If you are a leader reading this book, a step back and an honest diagnosis of your life would probably pinpoint an area or two where you have chased outward success, which may be overshadowing your true purpose. This realization isn't meant to elicit shame but rather present an opportunity to recalibrate toward the most important things.

So, how can you tell the difference? Success often feels like chasing the receipt that falls out of your car and blows across the parking lot. It keeps you pursuing the ultimate satisfaction that you think will come as a result, but it always seems just out of reach. Purpose, on the other hand, is steady and grounding. It brings peace that comes from knowing you are planting the right seeds, even if the fruit is not yet visible. Putting your focus in the right places allows you to invest in a life that will reap a harvest in the seasons ahead of you.

The Cost of Inaction

Most of us can agree that taking action is necessary in life. But many of us don't want to pay the required price—the energy, discomfort, or risk that is involved. However, what often gets overlooked is the *cost of inaction*, which quietly takes a much greater toll. When we stay settled in our comfort zones, we may save ourselves from short-term discomfort, but we sacrifice much more in the long run. Many do not realize the real cost of inaction, like staying stagnant, feeling regret, missing opportunities, and limiting our impact as a leader. The bottom line is that the pain of staying stuck far outweighs the discomfort of moving forward. This is why your vision and purpose must serve as the compass and fuel for your life, even in the small things. As Dr. Susan David, a Harvard psychologist writes, "Discomfort is the price of admission to a meaningful life" (David, 2020).

So, take a moment to reflect on your life. In what areas have you avoided taking an action you know is essential for your growth? It could be that you've left certain leadership challenges unaddressed—issues you know are your responsibility to confront, yet you've stayed silent. Maybe you've grown passive in your marriage, avoiding the hard conversations needed to bridge the growing disconnection between you and your spouse. You might be realizing that you've delayed becoming fully present at home, neglecting to invest your best energy where it ultimately matters most. Or perhaps you've quietly given up the fight against the anxiety and overwhelm that come with the weight you're carrying, choosing to cope rather than confront. These areas of inaction rarely happen without reason—there's often something deeper beneath the surface.

> **To understand what lies behind this inaction, start by asking yourself these questions:**
>
> 1. *What am I avoiding?*
>
> 2. *Why am I avoiding it? (What are the feelings holding me captive from taking action?)*

The root cause of inaction in our lives can come from many different areas, such as fears, feelings of inadequacy, self-sabotage, or limiting beliefs (Kallio, 2020). At these crossroads, the greater question emerges: *What will happen if I do nothing?*

> **Picture again the area of your life where you have not taken the action you should or need to take. Ask yourself:**
>
> 1. What will my life look like in three months if I don't act?
>
> 2. What could the result of my inaction be one year from now? Three years from now?
>
> 3. What will the cost of inaction be regarding my relationships, health, family, or leadership?

Once you have played out this scenario and assessed what the future consequence of your inaction could cost you, turn the questions around:

1. *What would my life look like in three months if I take daily action in this area?*

2. *What will the result be one year from now if I commit with clarity, discipline, and consistency? What about three years from now?*

3. *What will my marriage, health, family, or leadership look like if I brave the uncomfortable things and put in the work required to create the life I envision?*

When you look at your life from both perspectives—inaction *and* action—it creates a clearer landscape of what *you* can create. The growth you want is on the other side of what you are willing to pursue and your choices to make it happen. Progress occurs when your intentions and your actions become the *same thing*.

> Progress occurs when your intentions and your actions become the *same thing.*

6 Keys to Crafting Your Vision for Growth

Although there are many great books to guide you through the process of crafting a vision for your life, this book focuses on developing a vision for your *growth*. It is not solely about where you want to be five or ten years from now, but rather *who you want to become in the process*. Meaning, how you show up today, tomorrow, and the next with discipline and consistency. Because the sacrifice and commitment you put in today will determine the trajectory of your future. So, below are 6 keys to developing a vision that your future self would be proud of.

1. Evaluate Your Starting Point

To accurately map out where you want to go, you need to take an honest inventory of where you are currently at. Evaluate your strong points, weak areas, habits, and current circumstances. Ask yourself:

> *What areas of my life am I currently thriving in?*
> *Where do I feel stuck, stagnant, or discontent?*
> *What areas in my life do I need to change the way I "show up," and why is it essential that I do?*
> *What mindset or faulty systems in my life are holding me back from growing into the person I want to become?*

Your self-evaluation isn't about self-criticism. It is about self-awareness. Gaining clarity about your present situation lays the groundwork for you to build on.

2. Establish Your Growth Pillars

Rather than chasing abstract progress or an all-encompassing vision that many people default to, think about your growth as a structure supported by essential pillars, each representing a key area of your life. First, identify 3-4 core growth areas and reflect on those that feel vital to your personal development. These may include:

- Relationships: Marriage, children, family, and friendships
- Health/Wellness: Physical, emotional, and mental health
- Skills/Knowledge: Developing expertise and experiences in a specific area
- Habits/Schedule: Creating a disciplined and focused daily plan for execution

The objective is to create a vision with a targeted focus that will best set you up for the growth you are pursuing. As the law of diminishing returns indicates, the more focus areas there are, the less progress you are likely to see on *any* of them. Prioritize what matters most in the places you want to see the greatest return on your investment.

3. Define Your Outcomes

For each of the above pillars, articulate what success will look like. Ask yourself:

What will change in my life if I make meaningful, consistent progress in this area?

Example:

For *relationships*, the outcome might be: I will have a stronger, more connected marriage with my wife, where we both feel known, supported, and loved.

For *health/wellness*, the outcome might be: I will become stronger, have more mental clarity, increased energy, and invest in my longevity for the sake of my family.

For *skills/knowledge*, the outcome might be: I will become proficient in a specific skill over the next six months that will equip me to become a better leader or further my career.

For *habits/schedule*, the outcome might be: I will be intentional with my time each evening so that I don't become distracted with things that don't add value to my life and goals.

Once your outcomes are clearly established, you can then break them down into smaller, measurable, actionable steps, ensuring that each one feels achievable while still aligning with the bigger picture.

4. Identify Your Actionable Steps

Once your outcomes are defined, break them into actionable, bite-sized steps. These small wins build momentum. For instance:

- If your outcome is *building closer relationships*, your first step might be scheduling regular one-on-one time with key people in your life, like regular date nights with your spouse.
- If your goal is *improving wellness*, start by committing to 10 minutes of movement each morning rather than an intense, unsustainable regimen right out of the starting gate.

Remember, growth isn't about massive leaps, but daily, consistent progress. In chapter six, we will dive deeper into strategies for building effective, sustainable habits in your life.

5. Prioritize Progress Over Perfection

It is essential to recognize that growth rarely follows a straight line. You might miss a workout. You might feel disconnected from your spouse during a busy week. You might default for a few days into an old routine. Two keys to sustaining progress are *consistency* and *grace*. Every small step, even when imperfect, is a step closer to who you want to become. And when you misstep, give yourself the grace to get back on the path and keep moving forward. The process of growth is far from perfect. So, remind yourself: The process *is* progress.

6. Reflect and Recalibrate Regularly

Establish a time to regularly reflect on what is working, what is not, and what adjustments are needed. Sports coaches create a game plan before each match, but once the whistle blows and the game starts, they are continually making adjustments and tweaking their tactics based on the scenario in front of them. For example, if you know you are approaching a busy holiday season or going on vacation, some modifications may be needed to fit your schedule.

The more you dial in your "why," the more you will begin to feel when you have drifted off course. When this happens, do not get too caught up in what you are *not doing*, but instead, focus on realigning with your vision and stacking those small wins again. Creating your vision for growth provides you with clarity for your life. By identifying where you are, defining where you want to go, and taking intentional steps forward, you build a foundation for the change you want to see. Growth is not about rushing to a finish line and is undoubtedly not always polished and glamorous. It is about putting in the work, learning along the way, and building a life you are proud of - one action at a time.

Your Legacy

Your legacy is not simply about what you leave behind. Your legacy is about the impact that you create while you are here. It is the mark that you leave on the lives of the people who matter most, the values you embody, and the growth that in turn helps grow those around you.

When you choose to intentionally pursue your potential, you have the opportunity to transform your own life and also influence those around you. It is the rising tide that raises all ships. Think of your growth as planting seeds in the lives of others. Those seeds in your relationships, marriage, children, and those you lead will grow and continue to make an impact long after you are gone.

PAUSE AND REFLECT:

1. *What legacy do I want to leave among those I care about the most?*

2. *How will pursuing my potential shape the story that my life will leave behind?*

Imagine looking back on your life years from now, knowing that the hard things you chose to face, the limiting beliefs you conquered, and the resilience you showed in the challenging times didn't just change your trajectory, but also imprinted the lives of those closest to you. True legacy is not about success, accolades, or titles you have obtained. True legacy is about the lives you have changed because you chose growth over settling for comfort.

Who You're Becoming

Your vision and purpose are more than just passive goals or noble ideas. They are powerful forces that shape your growth, influence your decisions, and determine the legacy you leave in others. Like a compass and an engine, they provide both direction and momentum. You need them both so you can move forward with focus and intention.

Real clarity for growth comes when you stop asking, *What should I do?* and begin asking, *Who am I becoming?* From there, your vision comes alive by aligning your daily actions with a future you believe in. And if you feel off course along the way, step back and check the map. When you recalibrate and continue forward progress, even small steps add up over time.

In the upcoming chapter, we'll explore the power of taking full ownership and responsibility for your life, no matter the situation or circumstance. Because once you realize that *you* are the one who ultimately determines your outcome, every decision, habit, and thought begins to carry even greater significance.

LEADERSHIP IN ACTION: VISION AND PURPOSE

A vision for growth is essential in your personal life, but it is also the cornerstone of effective leadership. When you have a clear, compelling vision for the development of your team, it brings alignment and helps create an environment of collective accountability. This vision goes beyond words on a wall. It is about forward progress and tapping into the potential in both your people and your organization.

When people understand the "why" behind your vision for your team's growth, they are more likely to become engaged and invested. Share your vision consistently in meetings, one-on-one conversations, and through your actions. Clear communication is key—not just through emails, but how you show up daily. Provide others with experiences through mentorships and opportunities for development, and empower them in areas that align with their personal goals and those of the organization. As you equip and mobilize them with tools and experiences, you actively demonstrate your investment in who they can become.

Throughout my career, some of the most powerful conversations with those I lead have been through learning and understanding their passions and what drives them. Once I discovered what makes them "come alive," I could connect them with opportunities most aligned with those aspirations. This process of championing the growth of others and serving as a catalyst for their success has been one of my greatest joys as a leader. After all, the growth and development of *people* is the highest calling of leadership.

Your Pursuit of Growth:

1. Communicate your vision and purpose clearly and often, making it a part of everyday conversation. Furthermore, ensure the vision for your team's growth is understood and followed up with opportunities.
2. What gets measured gets managed. How do you actively measure progress and ensure you are moving toward the desired results? Spending time in regular, honest conversations with people about their growth keeps the conversation at the forefront. Furthermore, it provides a layer of personal accountability for each person on your team.

CHAPTER FOUR

Choose to Take Ownership

THE "UNCHARTED" FRAMEWORK
9 KEYS FOR PURSUING YOUR POTENTIAL IN LEADERSHIP AND LIFE

- **U** — UNDERSTAND YOUR LIMITING BELIEFS
- **N** — NAVIGATE WITH VISION AND PURPOSE
- **C** — CHOOSE TO TAKE OWNERSHIP
- **H** — HARNESS RESILIENCE
- **A** — ACT WITH DISCIPLINE AND CONSISTENCY
- **R** — REFRAME YOUR MINDSET
- **T** — TRANSFORM FAILURE INTO OPPORTUNITIES
- **E** — EMBRACE COMMUNITY AND ACCOUNTABILITY
- **D** — DARE TO CLIMB

David Goggins, known as one of the toughest endurance athletes and motivational speakers in the world, spent the first part of his life anything but successful. Growing up, Goggins faced extreme adversity. He endured an abusive household, struggled with poverty, battled obesity, and wrestled with his self-worth from years of trauma. Working as a pest exterminator in his twenties, he felt stuck, bitter, and convinced that life had dealt him an unfair hand. He lacked direction, and both his relationships and health were deteriorating.

But, one moment of brutal honesty forced him to confront the truth. As Goggins watched a documentary about the Navy SEALs, he realized that no one was going to rescue him from his circumstances. He had allowed himself to remain a victim of his past, and no one was responsible for his life except for him. He was the only one who could take ownership of his choices, his growth, and ultimately his future.

At this turning point in his life, he set the goal of joining the Navy SEALs. At nearly 300 pounds, Goggins faced the overwhelming odds of losing over 100 pounds in three months just to qualify. Instead of making excuses or blaming his situation, he chose relentless discipline and overhauled his mindset. He created a plan, committed to every nuance of his vision, and transformed his life physically and mentally (Goggins, 2018).

But Goggin's journey did not just stop with outward achievements. His newfound sense of ownership carried over into every aspect of his life. He mended broken relationships and set out to inspire others to take radical responsibility for how they show up each day.

The Shift from Excuses to Ownership

Goggins' story is a powerful example of what can happen when we take full ownership of our lives. He did not make excuses or wait for ideal conditions or external motivation. He started exactly where he was, acknowledged the choices that led him there, and made the commitment to change. The good news is that this power is inside of everyone. It's inside of *you*. Your growth is not handed to you. It's earned through taking responsibility for your life, relentless perseverance, and continual commitment.

Throughout this chapter, we will explore the differences between ownership and self-accountability, understand the value of cultivating self-awareness in our lives, and discover powerful tools for self-reflection. These instrumental shifts in mindset will create the foundation for you to take action so that your leadership and life can prosper in areas that once seemed out of reach.

The Partnership for Growth

As we begin this chapter, we must distinguish between two key concepts: *ownership* and *self-accountability*. Although often used interchangeably, each plays a unique role in shaping your mindset to lead yourself with excellence and intention. *Ownership* puts you in the driver's seat of your life, while *self-accountability* keeps you on the road.

Ownership: The Driver's Seat

Taking ownership is a mindset. It is about acknowledging that your life is *your* responsibility. It is the decision to fully embrace the actions and outcomes of your life, understanding that you are the one in your life's driver's seat. When you take ownership of your life, you no longer blame others or point fingers. This also means recognizing that your current circumstances, whether favorable or not, are yours to do something about.

For example, taking ownership of your health means you don't blame your hectic schedule for your lack of fitness. Instead, it means problem-solving, making the necessary adjustments, and owning the solution to the scenario in front of you. When you do this, you are recognizing that you are the one who makes things happen in your life rather than letting life happen to you.

While this might sound daunting to you as you look at life's current scenarios in front of you, it is also incredibly freeing. Shifting your mindset away from thinking that other people or situations have more control over your future than you do clears the path of excuses. It empowers you to live from a place of intentionality.

Former US Military Commander Jocko Willink, author of *Extreme Ownership* (Willink & Babin, 2015) has been a resounding voice for the importance of taking responsibility for your life and how you show up as a leader. In Willink's now-famous TEDTalk from 2017 (TED, 2017), he encapsulated the importance of ownership in every facet of life:

> *I say, take ownership. Take extreme ownership. Don't make excuses. Don't blame any other person or any other thing. Get control of your ego. Don't hide your delicate pride from the truth. Take ownership of everything in your world, the good and the bad. Take ownership of your mistakes. Take ownership of your shortfalls. Take ownership of your problems and then take ownership of the solutions that will get those problems solved. Take ownership of your mission. Take ownership of your job, of your team, of your future, and take ownership of your life.*

Taking ownership means acknowledging that *your life* is *your responsibility*.

Self-Accountability: Your Guardrails

Just as ownership is integral to your growth, so is self-accountability. Self-accountability is the inner commitment of answering for your decisions, actions, and the outcomes that follow. Although the word accountability is used often in leadership roles regarding answering to others, this refers to the crucial aspect of answering to *yourself*.

PAUSE AND REFLECT:

1. *Do I follow through with what I say I am going to do in my life?*

2. *Do I take responsibility for my actions (or inaction) in life?*

Self-accountability ensures you're not just setting goals but following through and making the necessary adjustments when you are not. The term *self-accountability* may be one you are unaccustomed to, because there is often more familiarity with the word *accountability*, regarding a personal support system comprised of a friend or mentor to give you honest feedback and encouragement. While this type of accountability is essential and will be discussed in a later chapter, self-accountability is the focus here. It is the proverbial mirror that you look in at the end of the day that requires you to answer the question: *Did I actually do what I said I was going to do?*

> Self-accountability asks the question: Did I actually do what I said I was going to do?

Self-Accountability in Action

Self-accountability is a mindset that requires commitment and follow-through, knowing that you must answer to yourself at the end of the day. It holds a standard of who you have resolved to become and does not let you settle for anything less. Below are 3 keys to ensuring self-accountability in your life.

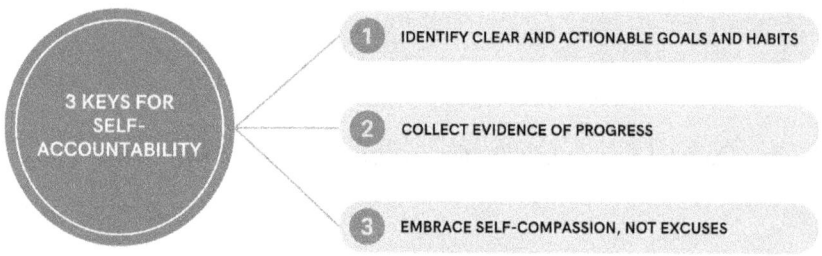

1. Establish Clear and Actionable Goals and Habits

You cannot hold yourself accountable for intentions that are vague or undefined. Establish specific, measurable goals for different areas of your life.

Action Tip: Break larger goals into smaller, manageable tasks with deadlines. For example, instead of saying, *I want to be healthier,* commit to walking thirty minutes daily or meal prep on Sunday for your week's worth of lunches.

2. Collect Evidence of Progress

Regularly evaluate your choices and monitor your actions to determine if you are following through with what you said you would do. Remember, it is about progress, not perfection. And a little progress each day adds up to significant results.

Action Tip: At the end of each week, ask yourself:
Did I follow through on my commitments? What is the evidence of it?
If not, what prevented me from it? What barriers do I need to address?

Tools like journals, habit trackers, or apps to record daily progress are great because they are visual evidence of staying true to your word and commitments.

3. Embrace Self-Compassion, Not Excuses
Do not let self-criticism mask itself as self-accountability. One leads to growth, while the other leads to shame. Instead, acknowledge the areas you find yourself off course, take responsibility, and create a plan for your next step. Remember that it is a daily process. Excuses are like quicksand to your progress. Once you start making them, you run the risk of only getting sucked in deeper. Those who take ownership eliminate excuses from their vocabulary.

Action Tip: Develop this mindset after setbacks:
This is what happened. This is what I'll do differently. And this is how I'll move forward.

The Cornerstone of Personal Responsibility

When seventy-five members of the Stanford Graduate School of Business Advisory Council were asked to identify the most critical skill for leaders to develop, their answer was overwhelmingly clear: it was self-awareness (George et al., 2007). Self-awareness is defined as the ability to see yourself clearly by recognizing and understanding your moods, drives, and emotions, as well as the impact you have on others. Additionally, it is the process whereby you continually develop an understanding of your talents, strengths, weaknesses, purpose, core values, beliefs, and desires (Gardner et al., 2005).

Self-awareness is the cornerstone to taking ownership and personal responsibility for our lives. As leaders, we are wired to diagnose issues, anticipate potential problems, and objectively evaluate multi-faceted situations to create systems and processes that move teams forward. However, when applying this in our personal lives, things can start feeling messier and even uncomfortable. This is because an honest reflection of our life may reveal areas we've avoided or settled into our comfort zones.

However, to truly grow, we must be willing to have those regular, truthful moments of reflection. We must be willing to look at our shortcomings and take a stand against the areas of passivity in our lives. When we determine who we want to become and then challenge our mindsets, systematic barriers, and the excuses we have embraced, we set ourselves up for success—to take the ground we are after.

Your "Home Inspection"

Cultivating self-awareness is like hiring a home inspector for your life. A home inspector's role is not to rebuild your house. Their role is to identify the hidden issues and structural weaknesses that need attention. Home inspectors do not sugarcoat problems or shift the blame. Their job is to uncover the truth so you can make informed decisions about repairs and improvements that will benefit both the short-term and long-term health of your home. Similarly, self-awareness helps you assess the "current condition" of your life:

- *Are there cracks in your mindset?*
- *Are there leaks in your emotional health?*
- *Are there outdated habits or thought patterns that need rewiring?*

Just as a homeowner cannot ignore structural flaws without risking more significant damage, you cannot afford to ignore the warning signs and areas in your life where you may be compromising your vision. Perhaps a crack in your "foundation" stems from a limiting belief such as, *I can never catch a break. Things never end up working out for me anyways, so why bother trying?* A self-awareness "inspection" of these thinking patterns may reveal that a victim mindset is holding you back because you feel that your external circumstances have more power over your life than you do. Taking ownership means identifying this belief and reframing your perspective toward things outside your control.

An "emotional leak" may look like recurring frustration about the growth in some of your relationships at work or home. Getting curious might reveal that you are struggling with unrealistic expectations, unforgiveness, or fears that keep you from being truly open, vulnerable, or connected. By recognizing the root and identifying the core emotions driving your behaviors, you can then take ownership of how *you* contribute to your relationships rather than blaming others or avoiding the issues altogether.

Next, think of your habits and systems of your life as your "wiring." Spending time in self-reflection might uncover that your morning scrolling habit drains your focus and productivity during your most critical hours of the day. Taking ownership of your life means acknowledging that this habit is not serving your goals and is distracting you and keeping you preoccupied with meaningless content. Instead, "rewire" your morning routine to center around what is most important to you, such as exercising, reading, or prayer.

Each of these examples represents how self-awareness helps you identify what needs attention in specific areas of your life. Additionally, by taking responsibility and ownership, you move beyond *awareness of these areas* and commit to *addressing these areas*. Just like a homeowner takes action after a detailed inspection.

Not More Things, But *Right* Things

A common theme throughout this book has been that there is more inside of you than you realize, and it is built only in the hard things you are avoiding. But it's vital to clarify that I'm not calling you to fill your life with *more things*. Instead, I'm calling you to build your life on the *right things*.

The later chapters around discipline, consistency, and mindset will contain plenty of strategies to equip you to suit up for battle and take the land that is rightfully yours. A key component of self-awareness, however, is recognizing which battles are the *right ones*, and which ones leave you (or others) wounded on the battlefield.

Having drive, grit, and tenacity are essential characteristics of a growth-minded leader, as long as you have a healthy gauge of how far you are pulled and in which direction. Your life may consist of a high-stakes leadership position, a team to steward, and most importantly, your family who relies on you. But, when you push yourself to maximum capacity without a healthy measure of self-awareness, you risk stretching yourself beyond your capacity to show up healthily in the areas that matter most. As you pursue growth in one area of your life, ensuring that the pendulum swings back when necessary is vital, always protecting the most important areas *first*.

When Ownership Creates Opportunity

In 2009, Leslie Scott was in her mid-40s and found herself at a crossroads. She was overcommitted at her six-figure job, which left her leaving each day emotionally depleted and frustrated with her unhealthy work environment. She was struggling as a single parent and lived with no shortage of fingers to point and blame to disperse for the state of her personal life. She knew her life needed an overhaul, but did not know where to start. So, she looked inward.

Leslie determined that only by taking ownership of her life could she move from living as a victim of her current situation toward creating the life she envisioned. Her growth did not start with outside changes, but rather on the *inside*. She decided to take a nine-month sabbatical and engage in deep, honest self-reflection. She spent time journaling to process her emotions and gain clarity for the next season of her life. These moments became a turning point for Leslie, and she took the leap to pursue her passion and build a bath and beauty company from scratch. Within a few short years, Walton Wood Farms had grown into a multi-million-dollar international brand (Sinrich, 2023).

The key to Leslie's growth? When faced with burnout, personal challenges, and feelings that her circumstances were outside her control, Leslie realized that no one else was going to step in and make the changes she needed. Instead, this was her responsibility, as scary as it may have seemed.

This story is not simply about a career pivot or business start-up. It is a testament to the catalyst that taking ownership can be in our lives. When we ask ourselves, *What am I willing to take responsibility for?* we begin to see the opportunity to blaze a new trail on the mountain, rather than only the fallen trees and impassable terrain.

> Your circumstances shape your starting point, but your choices will determine your trajectory.

The Value of Self-Reflection

An integral component of fostering self-awareness is the process of self-reflection. If self-awareness is the *what*, then self-reflection is the *how*. This powerful practice better equips you to take ownership of your life by taking the intentional time to pause, evaluate your thoughts/feelings/actions, and identify where you need to process or recalibrate. Without regular self-reflection, it is easy to default to autopilot or even remain unaware of the footholds keeping you stuck.

I spent much of my early leadership career living day-to-day, focused on the next task at hand, the next challenge in front of me, or the next goal I was chasing. What I didn't do was take the time to "check in" with myself and process what was really happening *inside of me.* This pattern led to blind spots in my life and perpetual unrest. I could not put language to the stress I was feeling, and my overwhelm felt like a wet blanket. It wasn't until I began to look inward and do the gritty work of asking myself honest questions that I was able to see the unprocessed emotions that I was continually avoiding.

One tool that became essential to my growth was the daily use of the *Core Emotion Wheel,* developed by Dr. Glenn and Phyllis Hill (Connection Codes, n.d.). The Core Emotion Wheel consists of eight core emotions that we often encounter throughout the day. By identifying where we experience them on a daily basis, we can understand how they are impacting our thoughts and ultimately our behaviors. The eight core emotions are:

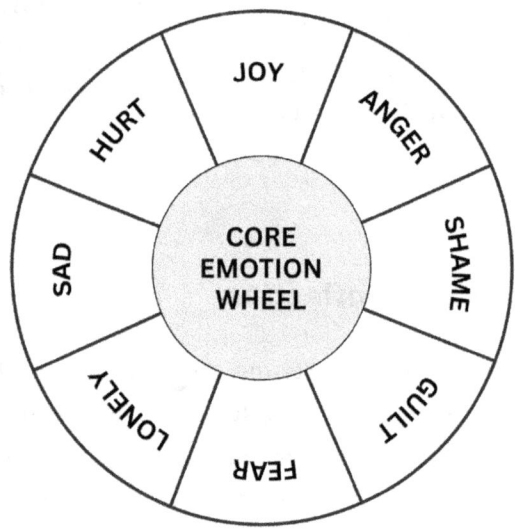

For example, every evening I take five minutes to reflect on each emotion by asking myself:

I felt hurt today when…
I felt fear today when…

I felt joy today when…
And so on.

After recognizing the emotions that I felt throughout the day, I can more clearly process what is going on inside me. I then assess the surrounding context, determine the accuracy of the situation, and identify if there is any more work that needs to be done. Most of the time, I am OK to move on. Other times, I need to take a few extra minutes to journal my thoughts or work through those emotions in more depth.

Overall, this simple yet powerful process has been vital to my growth. It prevents the "log jam" of emotions inside me that would not only be detrimental for me, but also for those I lead, care about, and want to show up emotionally healthy for.

It Starts with You

True ownership requires you to stop waiting for external circumstances to change and take responsibility for your own life. It is about acknowledging that while you cannot control everything, you *can* control your actions, your mindset, and your follow-through. Through building self-awareness, engaging in self-reflection, and holding yourself accountable to what you say you will do, you create the conditions for authentic and lasting change.

Growth doesn't happen by accident—it's the result of intentional, daily choices. As you move forward, embrace the responsibility of creating your future and remember that each step you take with ownership brings you closer to the person the world around you needs.

LEADERSHIP IN ACTION: OWNERSHIP

As a leader, taking ownership means accepting full responsibility for your actions and their outcomes. Did a decision not turn out how you envisioned it? Did your lack of foresight result in the need for a course correction or an adjusted strategy? If so, take responsibility for it. Own your mistakes openly rather than deflect them or make excuses. Hold yourself to the same standard you expect from those you lead. When mistakes happen, be the first to acknowledge your role in them.

Owning your situation in this way builds trust and credibility. It models that effective leadership is not based on having all the answers but rather on learning, adapting, and moving forward. When you model this level of ownership, you empower your team to do the same. You foster a culture where people are not afraid to take risks, innovate, or stretch themselves - because they understand all of it is necessary for growth.

Your Pursuit of Growth:

1. When you or your team find yourselves in a less-than-ideal situation, it is easy to default to blame—pointing fingers at circumstances, policies, or even other people. Blame might sound like, "...because we didn't have enough time," or "...because they didn't follow through." However, as a leader, you set the standard for how your team responds. Your reaction in these moments will either reinforce an environment of accountability or enable an environment of excuse-making.

Taking ownership supports the long-term growth of your team while pointing fingers hinders it.
2. Foster a culture of ownership by recognizing and celebrating individuals who take responsibility, show initiative, and are brave beyond their comfort zone. When people see that taking ownership is a prerequisite for growth, they are more likely to step out in self-belief.

CHAPTER FIVE

Harness Resilience

THE "UNCHARTED" FRAMEWORK
9 KEYS FOR PURSUING YOUR POTENTIAL IN LEADERSHIP AND LIFE

U	UNDERSTAND YOUR LIMITING BELIEFS
N	NAVIGATE WITH VISION AND PURPOSE
C	CHOOSE TO TAKE OWNERSHIP
H	HARNESS RESILIENCE
A	ACT WITH DISCIPLINE AND CONSISTENCY
R	REFRAME YOUR MINDSET
T	TRANSFORM FAILURE INTO OPPORTUNITIES
E	EMBRACE COMMUNITY AND ACCOUNTABILITY
D	DARE TO CLIMB

At fourteen years old, Erik Weihenmayer's world changed forever. Diagnosed with retinoschisis, he faced the scary reality of progressive blindness, ultimately losing his sight before graduating high school. For many, this kind of adversity would feel insurmountable and a reason enough to let go of their life's aspirations. But, Erik's response was different. He refused to be a victim of his diagnosis, and let resilience become his defining characteristic.

Instead of letting blindness limit him, Erik strengthened his other senses and doubled down on his goals. Wrestling became his outlet, where he represented his high school team in the Iowa State Wrestling Championships, proving that resilience can overcome even the most significant obstacles.

After his high school years, Erik grew passionate about rock climbing. His resilience and mindset led him to one of the greatest achievements and feats no person in history had previously accomplished. He became the first blind person to scale the summit of Mount Everest (No Barriers, n.d.). But for Erik, it was never just about reaching the mountain's highest peak. It was about proving what is possible when you refuse to let life's obstacles define you.

Erik went on to co-found the organization, *No Barriers*, which inspires others to embrace adversity as a tool for transformation. Its motto, "What's within you is stronger than what's in your way" (No Barriers, n.d.) serves as a call to action to face life's challenges head-on, regardless of the mountain standing in front of you.

Why Resilience Matters

Resilience is more than just bouncing back from hardships. Resilience is about leaning in, moving forward, and growing stronger as a result. It is not just about *surviving* adversity but also about *using* it as a catalyst for growth. Life is unpredictable, often hitting us with challenges that we never anticipated. Sometimes, it is a moment that knocks us off our feet. Other times, it is seasons of hardship, heartache, or the heaviness of an uphill battle. What separates those who grow and thrive from those who merely survive is the ability to adapt, endure, and grow stronger in the face of those challenges.

> **Resilience is more than just bouncing back from hardships. Resilience is about leaning in, moving forward, and growing stronger as a result.**

Resilience is not a trait we are born with. It develops from our courage to take the hits, steady ourselves, and continue to move forward. And, like any muscle that we want to grow stronger, it is developed through every uncomfortable repetition, even when the fatigue begins to set in. The APA Dictionary of Psychology defines resilience as:

> *The process and outcome of successfully adapting to difficult or challenging life experiences, especially through mental, emotional, and behavioral flexibility and adjustment to external and internal demands (American Psychological Association, 2018).*

In other words, when the going gets tough, our outcomes are determined by whether we face the storm head-on and grow stronger in the process, or allow ourselves to get battered by the wind and rain, left to clean up the debris. One forges us forward, the other leaves us stuck.

This chapter will uncover how to develop the fortitude to withstand those very obstacles you face and use them as steppingstones for your life. If growth is the journey, resilience is the traction that will move you through the rockiest parts of the path.

Don't Waste Your Hard Season

We need trials in our lives. We need times that will necessitate us to build resilience and perseverance. As uncomfortable and counterintuitive as that may sound, *without trials* we miss out on the opportunity to develop the character and strength necessary for growth.

In the fall of 2023, I was going through a difficult and emotionally trying time in my life. I was dealing with the unexpected loss of my biological father, with whom I had a distant and tumultuous relationship my entire life. The pain of a lifetime of dysfunction, combined with my present reality of emotions, felt despairing as I navigated the ensuing logistics and family dynamics.

One day, I was traveling down the interstate to the home where my father had lived. My heart and mind were heavy from the weight of the loss and the grief of accompanying strained family relationships. So, I decided to call my brother-in-law, Steve, to process what was going on inside me. While on the phone, I was having a bit of a "pity party." While I was expecting him to respond with, "Oh man, that sounds so hard," he instead paused and asked me a simple question: "So, what lesson is there for you to learn in this?"

> Within every hardship is an invitation for growth. Within every obstacle is an opportunity. Don't waste your hard season.

I sat silent on the phone, slightly taken aback by his reply. He then said, "There's a lesson for you in this that you wouldn't have the opportunity to learn if you weren't going through it. However, you get to make the choice whether you learn it or not."

While this was far from the advice I hoped for, it was the truth I needed at that moment. In every trial, there is an opportunity. If you don't go through challenging situations, you won't have the opportunity to learn the lessons necessary for growth. It didn't lessen the pain I felt in the moment, but it shifted my perspective about the season I was facing. We all go through hard seasons, difficult times, failure, and loss. It is how we respond, however, that makes all the difference.

PAUSE AND REFLECT:

What are you currently going through in your life that you need to reframe your perspective on? What area do you feel is overwhelming and something you would rather avoid?

Ask yourself:

1. *What lesson is there for you to learn in the midst of it?*

2. *Where is the invitation to grow?*

Opportunities in Disguise

In the 2007 film *Evan Almighty* (Shadyac, 2007), Evan Baxter, played by Steve Carell, was a news reporter from Buffalo, New York. Early in the movie, Baxter was elected to Congress. Soon after being elected, "God"—played by Morgan Freeman—visited Baxter and charged him with building an ark for an impending flood in their region, which was currently experiencing widespread drought.

During Baxter's journey, he experienced discouragement, relational disconnection, and self-doubt while embarking on the monumental project. Amid his strained relationships and waning belief in his ability to move forward, God (Morgan Freeman) shared with Baxter the key to growth in his life–the breakthrough he was looking for would be found in his willingness to view the situations in front of him as *opportunities* presented to him. It was all about perspective. Freeman goes on to say:

> *If someone prays for patience, do you think God gives them patience? Or does he give them the opportunity to be patient? If he prayed for courage, does God give him courage, or does he give him opportunities to be courageous? If someone prayed for his family to be closer, do you think God zaps them with warm fuzzy feelings, or does he give them opportunities to love each other?*

These words—coming from a 2000s family comedy—hit true to the core. In our lives, there is no smooth path over the mountain. The things we desire to see in our lives require effort. The relationships we long for require sacrifice. The vision we have requires perseverance. And, the growth necessary for us to become leaders who truly impacts the lives of others requires daily commitment. Remember, the rocks in your path might just be opportunities in disguise to gain better traction for your climb.

Circling the Mountain

When we don't learn the lesson, we go through it again. The uncomfortable truth is that our growth in these areas is on the other side of *leaning into the lesson*.

Have you ever found yourself facing the same kinds of challenges over and over as if you are circling the same mountain? When you

HARNESS RESILIENCE

avoid the situation, numb the pain, or shift blame to others, it might provide temporary relief. The challenge itself, however, does not disappear. Instead, it often reappears in new relationships, different jobs, or unexpected moments.

These moments are not just coincidence or "bad luck." They are usually an *invitation*. They expose the gaps in our maturity and the places we need to grow. So, when we resist confronting the situation, the mountain does not simply go away. Instead, we end up returning to the same struggles again, just in a new scenario. Unfortunately, there is no shortcut over the mountain. Growth does not occur when we sidestep the hard things. It happens when we confront them. Imagine the outcome if you reframe your perspective from, *"Here we go again"* to, *"This is my chance. I am not going to miss it."*

Your perspective makes all the difference. When you encounter a familiar challenge or find yourself negatively responding to a situation, ask yourself:

What part of my growth is waiting for me here?

The process is anything but easy. When you have been avoiding the climb, it takes courage to take the first step forward, and resilience to keep going when the path feels steep. It requires introspection, discipline, and even forgiveness at times. However, when we choose to stop circling the same mountain and start climbing, we find that the struggles we once avoided have the potential to shape us into someone stronger, with greater maturity, and equipped with better tools to tackle the next one.

> When you encounter adversity, ask yourself: *What part of my growth is waiting for me here?*

Every mountain you face in life has a purpose. It is to prepare you and propel you into your potential.

Avoiding the mountain leaves you at the lower elevations, which comes with frustration, discouragement, and a victim mentality. On the other hand, climbing the mountain builds hope and resilience, and sets an example for others to follow.

The Stockdale Paradox

Admiral James Stockdale's story, famously recounted in *Good to Great* by Jim Collins (Collins, 2001), is a profound testament to resilience. Admiral Stockdale was a prisoner of war in Vietnam for over seven years, where he endured terrible physical and mental suffering. During his time as a prisoner, he persevered by developing a mindset that gave him the strength to overcome some of the harshest conditions imaginable. His approach, now known as the "Stockdale Paradox," serves as a framework for fostering resilience in the face of adversity.

The Stockdale Paradox embodies the delicate balance between two concepts: *unwavering faith* and *brutal honesty*. Stockdale explained that while he never lost faith that he would ultimately overcome his circumstances, he also refused to shy away from the painful realities of his situation. He famously stated, "You must never confuse faith that you will prevail in the end—which you can never afford to lose—with the discipline to confront the most brutal facts of your current reality, whatever they might be."

Faith is the belief required to persevere without visible evidence of the outcome. It is built upon inner conviction, hope, and steadfastness. On the other hand, *honesty* is the clear-eyed, objective acceptance of the challenges or setbacks you are facing, without denying the reality of the situation. Whether it's a personal setback, a professional failure, or a seemingly insurmountable obstacle, the Stockdale Paradox is a challenge to confront the "honest, brutal facts" of where we are, while maintaining faith in where we can go.

> **PAUSE AND REFLECT:**
>
> 1. *Brutal Honesty:* Reflect on a current situation in your life. What challenges or barriers are you facing? What hard truths do you need to acknowledge before you can move forward?
>
> 2. *Unwavering Faith:* What is your source of faith and hope? What future vision sustains you in continuing to push forward?

Normalizing Difficulties

We often approach life with an unspoken expectation that things should go smoothly and that our relationships, careers, and personal growth will follow a steady, upward trajectory. Unfortunately, this expectation can set us up for disappointment when challenges inevitably arise. When difficulties come, they can feel like an injustice or even a blindside hit that leaves us disoriented and discouraged. However, struggles are not anomalies. They are a normal part of life.

Trials are unavoidable, and even the most perfectly laid plans come with hardships. But, when we begin normalizing difficulties in our lives, we are more equipped to stand firm and not be shaken. Our feet are firmly planted in the understanding that storms may come, but the clouds will also give way to clearer skies. This mindset shift can make all the difference in our lives.

This is a lesson that Ken Claytor, speaker and pastor of Alive Church in Orlando, Florida shared after a profound conversation with his counselor:

I was talking to my counselor, and he asked how everything was going.

And I was like, "Well you know, this is happening in my marriage, this is happening with our kids, our church people, this is what's happening with our finances, and I just started telling him all the negative stuff. I vented."

And he said, 'Your problem is that you just want life to be easy and you don't expect any difficulties.' And he said, 'People who don't expect difficulties end up overeating and over-drinking because they just want to be happy or they idolize happiness.'

Then my counselor said, 'But Jesus, in God's word, never promised us an easy life. He never said there wouldn't be difficulties. As a matter of fact, he said the opposite. He said as long as you are in this world, you will have… difficulties. But then He said, 'Be of good cheer, because I have overcome the world.'"

And what dawned on me is that His grace is sufficient for us in difficulties. No matter what you go through, whether it be menopause, financial things, whether it be something in your marriage, whatever is happening, God never promised us that we would not go through difficulties. He just promised us that He would be with us in the midst of our difficulties.

So my answer for people would be that we have to normalize difficulties. What you are going through - we have to normalize this. When people leave your life, they ghost you, we have to normalize this. You can't just be sucker-punched every single time you go through a battle. Like, 'Why is this happening to me?' Like something strange is happening (Clator, 2024).

Ken's counselor offered a significant truth: difficulties are not an interruption to life. They are a *part of life*. Difficulties are the spaces where your character is developed and your leadership is refined. As a leader in your workplace, home, or community, you will face challenges that test your patience and resolve. Look at these challenges as your training ground. Great leaders do not avoid difficulties but face them with the intention of growing as a result.

6 Keys for Developing Resilience

The theme of this chapter is that resilience is not something we are innately born with but, rather, is built by choice. You have an opportunity to brush yourself off and continue the ascent or to retreat down the mountain. One will grow you, and the other will slow you. Below are six practical keys and reminders for developing resilience in your life:

1. **Embrace the Hard Things**

    Growth happens in the *discomfort* zone. Choose to face challenges rather than avoid them, recognizing that each difficulty is an opportunity to strengthen your character and expand your capacity.

2. **Reframe Your Perspective**

Shift your mindset from seeing challenges as obstacles to viewing them as opportunities for growth. Ask yourself: *What can I learn from this? How will this make me stronger?*

3. **Develop Daily Disciplines**

Cultivate habits that ground you. Whether journaling, physical exercise, or moments of mindfulness and prayer, these daily practices build inner strength and help you stay anchored when life inevitably gets tough. This will be discussed more in the next chapter.

4. **Normalize Difficulties**

Expect setbacks and failures as part of the process, not as evidence that you are on the wrong path. Resilience develops when you keep going, despite temporary setbacks.

5. **Celebrate Small Wins**

Progress, no matter how small, is still progress. Acknowledge the small victories along the way to keep momentum and reinforce the resilience you are forming.

6. **Focus on Your Vision**

Keep your eyes on the bigger picture. Let your purpose and vision for growth fuel your perseverance through the challenges.

Built in the Battle

Resilience is what enables you to grow stronger with each challenge. Every time you choose to lean in, you build something deeper in your character. As adversity stretches you, resilience teaches you that discomfort isn't something to run from, but something to grow through. Your limits aren't fixed, and you have the choice to expand your capacity beyond what you once thought possible.

Your resilience is forged in the moments when you choose to keep going when quitting would be easier. It's in the decision to keep leading with integrity even when it costs you. And it's fortified in the quiet, unseen battles where no one else is watching—but you stay standing anyway. These things that feel like they might disqualify you are often the very catalysts that will propel you toward your potential.

In the next chapter, we will explore how discipline and consistency can turn your resilience into lasting results. It is one thing to stand firm in moments of difficulty, but it is another thing to make the day-in, day-out commitment to keep showing up. This next phase of growth requires you to engage fully and stay consistent—for the sake of who you are becoming and the legacy you're building.

LEADERSHIP IN ACTION: RESILIENCE

As a leader, you are the architect of your team's culture. Your resilience in the face of uncertainty, conflict, or change can either bolster or break your team's morale and forward progress. Reflect on a recent challenge you encountered in your leadership—perhaps a crisis, an unexpected setback, or a tough decision. Did you react impulsively, or did you lean in and respond confidently? Did your team feel your assurance amid uncertainty, or did they experience doubt and discouragement from you?

Developing steadfastness as a leader allows you to be the steady rudder, even in the middle of the strongest storms. Ultimately, your ability to reframe setbacks as growth opportunities will shape how your team approaches adversity. When they see you push forward with clarity and composure, you model for them to do the same. When resilience becomes a shared mindset, your team's collective perspective becomes responsive rather than reactive to whatever situation may arise.

Your Pursuit of Growth:

1. Lead by example. How you handle challenges sets the tone for your team. Before reacting emotionally, pause to collect your thoughts and assess the situation with the necessary perspective. Your ability to remain unwavering under pressure will build confidence in those you lead.

2. Develop a culture that embodies resilience. Provide opportunities for your team to reflect on setbacks together. Encourage them to ask, "What can we learn from this?" Or, "How do we move forward, stronger?" When obstacles are processed collectively with this perspective, it builds unity, develops perseverance, and strengthens your team as a byproduct.

CHAPTER SIX

Act with Discipline and Consistency

THE "UNCHARTED" FRAMEWORK
9 KEYS FOR PURSUING YOUR POTENTIAL IN LEADERSHIP AND LIFE

U	UNDERSTAND YOUR LIMITING BELIEFS
N	NAVIGATE WITH VISION AND PURPOSE
C	CHOOSE TO TAKE OWNERSHIP
H	HARNESS RESILIENCE
A	ACT WITH DISCIPLINE AND CONSISTENCY
R	REFRAME YOUR MINDSET
T	TRANSFORM FAILURE INTO OPPORTUNITIES
E	EMBRACE COMMUNITY AND ACCOUNTABILITY
D	DARE TO CLIMB

As a founding father and accomplished inventor, Benjamin Franklin is one of the most well-known figures in American history. However, perhaps one of Franklin's most important inventions was *himself*. Hundreds of years after his life, our country is still influenced by his accomplishments. People might not realize, though, that the foundation of his work and success was the commitment to his personal growth each day.

In his early 20s, Franklin realized that he had more potential than he was currently experiencing and desired to become a better version of himself—both in his career and character. As a result, he developed a system to track and build habits that aligned with his vision for personal growth. One of Franklin's profound insights was understanding that discipline was not just about what you consistently *do every day*, but *who you consistently are each day* (Ionescu, 2021). As a result, he created a list of thirteen virtues, including temperance (self-control), humility (character development), order (optimizing systems in his life), industry (eliminating distractions), and resolution (following through).

Each week, Franklin focused on one virtue, tracking his thoughts and actions in a journal to hold himself accountable. He established his goal, focused on his daily behaviors, measured his growth, and course-corrected when necessary. As Franklin famously said, "Energy and persistence conquer all things" (Wood & Hornberger, n.d.).

Franklin's powerful life accomplishments still impact our world today, and the backbone of it all was his personal commitment and discipline—day in and day out, when no one was watching.

A Disciplined Life

Discipline is the ability to make intentional choices and take consistent action toward our goals, even when the process feels tedious or boring. We all love to do the things we want to do. But discipline requires us to do the things *we need to do*. In other words, discipline is about being in charge of yourself and your choices, while denying yourself the easier path that does not serve your goals. When you can choose comfort *or* make the uncomfortable choices that lead to your growth, which one do you choose?

Sitting on the couch in the evening and watching another episode of *The Office* is easy. It takes discipline to go exercise at your gym or in your basement for thirty minutes, instead.

Sleeping in on a Saturday morning is easy. It takes discipline to wake up at 5:30 a.m. to read, quiet yourself, and prepare for the day.

Avoiding processing your emotions and not thinking about them is easy. It takes discipline to take the time to pay attention to what is really going on inside of you.

Eating comfort foods or finding the nearest drive-through for your next meal is easy. It takes discipline to eat healthy foods and fuel your body with optimal nutrition.

Letting life happen and going through the motions in your marriage, subtly shifting into disconnection is easy. It takes discipline to prioritize daily connection and make intentional time to grow your relationship.

Although comfort may seem easy for a time, the long-term toll on our health, relationships, and leadership may be much greater than we realize.

Discipline Over Motivation

Disciplined people are not led by their emotions. They are led by their vision. They are led by the person they want to become. Motivation is a fleeting feeling and an unreliable source for your growth. It is present in the highs but often fades when things get busy, distracting, or demanding.

On the other hand, discipline does not rely on how we feel in the moment. It is rooted in our commitment to our vision and the action necessary to progress towards it—regardless of how we "feel." Having a disciplined mindset is telling yourself, *I am going to do what I don't want to do, but I am going to do it as if I love to do it.*

Think of motivation as a spark. It can help light the fire but is not enough to keep it burning. Discipline, however, is the steady fuel that sustains your progress long after the excitement fades. Have you ever had a moment, idea, or endeavor that you felt a spark of motivation to tackle? Yet, a short time later, once the excitement wanes and the real work is required, your efforts taper off. Therein lies the difference between the *emotion of motivation* and the *mindset of discipline.*

There will be days when you will not feel like doing the hard things. You will not feel like getting up early, making the difficult decision, or staying focused. But, those are the moments when discipline steps in. That is when you stack the small wins against the easy choices that try to talk you into staying comfortable. In those moments, you must tell yourself, *My future self is worth the sacrifice I am making as my current self.* When you capture this vision, the price you pay will always pale in comparison to the life you are building.

For example, consider every action, no matter how small, as a deposit into a bank account. This bank account is the leader, parent, spouse, and person we desire to become. Every dollar, and even every penny, adds up over time. The power of discipline is that it generates *compound* interest. Consistent action over time multiplies into a life *you are leading*, rather than one leading you.

> A disciplined life is led by vision, not by emotions.

Consistency: The Name of the Game

It is not what you occasionally do that makes a difference. It is what you *consistently* do that matters over time. Steve Magness, best-selling author and performance coach, shared his insights from his research on the growth of college runners (Magness, 2024):

> *A few years ago, I tracked the improvement rates of my college runners and compared it to a whole slew of factors to see if anything correlated. The most important factor? If they showed up to practice. Those who missed the fewest days tended to improve the most.*
>
> *What's the best predictor of your grades in college? Not SAT scores, High School GPA, or your study time and habits. It's whether you show up. Attendance is one of the best predictors of academic performance. The same goes for any pursuit. Showing up is the most important part of performing.*
>
> *The hard thing isn't the fancy workout routine or the perfect training system. It's showing up consistently, day after day, month after month. Stacking solid work for a really long time.*
>
> *Show up, no matter what. Day after day. Sit down and write. Get out and exercise. Whatever the task you're trying to master, just keep showing up. If you show up enough, you'll get better. Consistency is the name of the game.*

> **PAUSE AND REFLECT:**
>
> **Think about the important areas in your life—those that you desire to continue growing in.**
>
> 1. *When it comes to your effort and discipline, are there any gaps in consistency?*
>
> 2. *What is getting in your way?*
>
> 3. *What practical adjustments do you need to make in your life?*

Consistency is not glamorous, and it is rarely easy. But consistency is where the transformation happens. The unseen, repetitive work you do when no one is watching will separate you from those who simply *aspire* for a better and more impactful life. As NBA legend Michael Jordan once said, "Champions don't become champions when they win an event, but in the hours, weeks, and years they spend preparing for it" (Thomas, 2024). If you want to win in your leadership, relationships, or health, there are simply no shortcuts.

ACT WITH DISCIPLINE AND CONSISTENCY

A Wake-Up Call

In December 2014, my friend and former college roommate, James Appleton, texted me. Just three months prior, he and his wife welcomed their first baby into the world, which served as a wake-up call for his life. I remember our conversation as he vulnerably shared that he had not prioritized his health, had no standard for his life, and that his habits reflected it.

> It is not what you *occasionally* do that makes a difference. It is what you do *consistently* that matters over time.

He shared that his wife looked at him a few nights prior and said, "What is your end game here? We have a daughter now." She was not simply referring to his 300-pound weight, but the fact that he was not the leader and example his household needed in this new season of life. Although her words stung, they were the very words he needed to hear.

In that moment everything started to change inside of James as he began to capture vision for his life. He knew that to create lasting, sustainable growth, he needed to build a new foundation, starting with his mindset. So, he identified the habits that kept him tethered to complacency and created a blueprint with seven commitments that he would embed into his life each day, targeting areas like physical activity, continuous learning, spiritual growth, and relational connection. He built trust in himself by doing the daily work necessary, whether he felt like it or not. As James put it:

> *I knew I needed to just start showing up each day, regardless of my emotions or the temptation to fall victim to my old habits. I realized that discipline is a daily choice, formed by pressing forward, rain or shine, sick or healthy, whether I am in the mood or not. This created a standard for my life. One that I was not going to compromise.*

Fast forward to today, James is an avid hiker and mountain guide who has lost over one hundred pounds and is committed to inspiring others to take ownership of their own lives with discipline and purpose. As a result of this passion, he has built a personal development coaching business called *Seek to Do More*, which has influenced thousands of people to become "stronger versions of themselves for the mountains and in life" (Seek to Do More, n.d.).

Your Future Self Will Thank You

Research shows that self-discipline is a far more significant predictor of success than factors like talent or intelligence. A study from the University of Pennsylvania found that self-control, a core component of discipline, was one of the most substantial predictors of academic success and life satisfaction. In fact, the study noted that people who were disciplined achieved higher levels of success in almost every aspect of life, from relationships to finances to career advancement (Duckworth & Seligman, 2005).

Additionally, a study by the American Psychological Association found that self-discipline is more important than IQ when it comes to achieving long-term goals. Meaning, while talent or intellectual abilities might get you started, the consistent effort and commitment each day drives lasting growth in your life (American Psychological Association, 2012).

It is no secret that life is filled with distractions and daily crossroads. Experts estimate that we make over 35,000 decisions per day (Krockow, 2018). Yes, you read that right. Many of these decisions are made without us even realizing it. Yet, others seem to challenge us day in and day out. Some decisions are inconsequential to our lives, such as, "What should I wear?" Other choices, however, keep us in constant tension between growth and comfort.

For example, look at the daily decisions on the chart below, which compare a life of "discipline" to a life of "comfort." Now, think of them as a math equation. Imagine their impact—positive or negative—if you add them up over weeks, months, or even years. What would your life look like as a byproduct?

A "DISCIPLINED" LIFE	A "COMFORTABLE" LIFE
Wake up early to be productive (journal, pray, etc.)	Hit the snooze button
Exercise for thirty minutes (lifting, walking, strength training)	Watch another TV show
Process your emotions for the day (Core Emotion Wheel)	Avoid them and "stuff" them down
Read and invest in your personal development	Sit and scroll on social media
Serve others, volunteer, and think "bigger" than yourself	Focus only on what benefits you
Have the uncomfortable but necessary conversations	Deflect the person or situation
Cook fresh, healthy foods for your meals	Eat empty, processed foods
Engage in hobbies and prioritize rest to deal with stress	Cope with alcohol, etc.
Be present in your home with your family after work	Continue to check your phone
Intentionally build connection in your relationships	Go through the motions

Settling for comfort now will only lead to discomfort later. Your influence as a leader, your physical health, your relationships, and your emotional health will ultimately pay the price. While this is not an exhaustive list, it is a snapshot of the many crossroads we face each day. Stack them up over time and one column is primed to win, while the other column settles for average. However, the fact that you are reading this book says that average is no longer an option for you.

Comfort: Your Cozy Prison

The ultimate goal of life is not to avoid discomfort. Read that again. Focusing on avoiding every pothole in life leaves you weary from playing it safe and ultimately settling for mediocrity. Most things in our society are hyper-focused on convenience—the quickest, the easiest, and the most comfortable option. While this may serve a purpose for some aspects of life regarding efficiency or effectiveness, in most cases, it is the antithesis of true and lasting personal growth.

A life of comfort is like a cozy prison. The longer you linger in comfort, the harder it becomes to leave. It desensitizes you and lulls you away from taking the leap toward the things that might initially feel scary. Its deception will keep you stuck, convincing you that it is in your best interest. However, no thriving relationship, innovation, or meaningful progress toward your goals will ever be achieved through avoiding discomfort. The path to growth and success includes pursuing the hard things and enduring resistance along the way, which shape and sharpen you to your fullest potential.

According to novelist Andre Gide, "Man cannot discover new oceans unless he has the courage to lose sight of the shore" (Gide, n.d.). For some, keeping sight of the shore and the illusion of safety may seem logical or even like wisdom to the rational mind. Oftentimes, fear disguises as "wisdom" and stagnation disguises as "security." The reality is that most people do not want to stay where they are at; deep down they desire to pursue their potential. However, many remain in their comfort zones because of underlying lies they subconsciously believe, such as:

I am afraid to fail, so it's safer not to try.
I don't think I actually have what it takes.
I've been rejected before, so it will just happen again.
I am waiting for the "right time" to start.
I am not ready yet.
I am fine where I am.

In actuality, staying comfortable in life is just a slow way of falling behind. Comfort creates the illusion that you have all the time in the world, or that the easier path is the logical one. But a day going through the motions is one less available day for the connection you seek, the dreams in your heart, and the purpose for which you are created. There will never be a "perfect time" to start anything. But like the old proverb says, "The best time to plant a tree was twenty years ago. The next best time is now."

Your story is not written in your comfort zone. It is written in the courage of action, even amidst the struggle. It is written in your overcoming of fears. It is written one bold decision at a time. Remember, courage in one person might look different in another, which is why it's *your* story. So, what kind of story are you writing?

The Neuroscience of Doing Hard Things

When it comes to living a disciplined life, more is happening in our brains than just our willpower. According to neuroscientist and podcaster Andrew Huberman, disciplining ourselves to do the hard things we would rather not do can actually make us stronger and even improve our longevity (Huberman, 2021). Huberman has highlighted the powerful connection between engaging in challenges and the Anterior Midcingulate Cortex (aMCC), a region of the brain responsible for our tenacity, our resistance to temptation, and our resilience. This part of the brain is activated and grows larger when we take on those challenges and push through discomfort. The more we exercise this part of the brain, the more we can develop the mental and emotional strength necessary to reach our goals.

For example, people who discipline their lives to optimize their health *grow* their aMCC. In contrast, people with obesity and who live sedentary lives have been found to have a *smaller* aMCC. This means every time you push yourself to complete a task you would rather avoid, learn a new skill, or commit to your growth-minded habits, you are actually neurologically and physiologically developing your brain in lasting ways.

Studies on the aMCC even suggest that a disciplined life of doing hard things has been linked to longevity, reduced stress, and enhanced long-term cognitive health. In other words, when you deny yourself the easy things now and live with the end goal in mind, you are literally building yourself to last.

So, what does this look like in your daily life? It's waking up early to exercise when you would rather stay in bed. It's saving the money instead of making an impulse purchase. It's even leaning into the difficult conversations you would prefer to avoid. Whatever the challenge is, let it have a greater purpose in your life than what is simply in front of you.

If a Man Works Hard, the Land Will Not be Lazy

In Malcom Gladwell's book *Outliers* (Gladwell, 2008), he highlights research on the value of discipline and consistency, and the growth that occurs as a byproduct. In Gladwell's book, he explores the work ethic of different farming cultures around the world. During the 1800's, many European farming cultures were characterized by brief episodes of

ACT WITH DISCIPLINE AND CONSISTENCY

work, followed by long periods of idleness. Most work took place from springtime through autumn. This mindset of working when optimal and "hibernating" when inconvenient resulted in a sedentary lifestyle, settling for less than what they had the capacity and potential for.

In contrast, throughout Southern China, farmers didn't "sleep" through the winter. Their work never ended. There was preparation for the following spring, creative side work, and deliberate action taken to ensure that the goals for their family and the village were met. Workers were unencumbered by the changing of the seasons, and, instead, they adapted and adjusted their approach toward prosperity. Their vision drove them, so they found a way through living with extreme discipline. The farmers lived with a mentality of, "If a man works hard, the land will not be lazy."

Furthermore, perhaps the most telling aspect of their mindset was the Chinese proverb, "No one who can rise before dawn three hundred sixty days a year fails to make his family rich."

PAUSE AND REFLECT:

1. *In what ways have you slipped into a season of idleness pertaining to your growth?*

2. *What area of your life's "land" needs tending? Where have the weeds grown or is your ground covered by snow?*

Too often, when the circumstances don't seem fit for planting seeds, the bigger picture of the harvest is lost. But the harvest you will reap *begins* with the mindset you are willing to sow. Let the winter seasons of your life create urgency for growth, rather than apathy and hibernation.

Show Me Your Calendar, and I'll Tell You Your Priorities

There are endless demands for our attention and our time. Another way of saying this is that there are endless *distractions* that can easily pull us off course. This is why it is crucial to build the rhythms of our lives in a way that protects our priorities.

If empowering those you lead is a priority, how many times in the last year have you released authority, trusted your people to make decisions, and released them to run with their ideas?

If you say health and fitness are priorities, where is it consistently showing up in your schedule?

If you say connection with your spouse is a priority, but there is no date night written on your calendar in the next month, is it *really* a priority?

Hope is not a strategy. Great ideas without action do not move the needle forward. And good intentions without focused pursuit usually end up in feelings of guilt or shame. One way to get an accurate picture of your priorities is to objectively look at your life through the lens of another person. Ask yourself:

If another person observed my schedule and actions for one week, what would they say are my priorities?

When we go through life as the "main character" of our story, it can be difficult to hold ourselves accountable. But when we zoom back to a one-hundred-foot view and take an honest evaluation, it can help reveal the places where we are cutting corners or the areas where we are out of alignment. Another great way to identify areas where you have compromised your priorities is to look at your life as the main character of a movie. As author Sahil Bloom (Bloom, 2025) frames it, "If I were the main character in a movie of my life, what would the audience be screaming at me to do right now?"

Boundaries

Self-discipline is more than just what you say "yes" to. It is equally about having the courage to say "no" to what distracts from your true priorities. One key to self-discipline is establishing healthy *boundaries* in your life. Boundaries serve as both the internal and external mechanisms that keep out things that don't serve your priorities, while simultaneously protecting them from the things that drain you, steal your peace, and vie for your attention.

What boundaries do you need to establish or recalibrate in your life? Maybe it's a relational boundary with someone who does not add value to the direction you are pursuing. Maybe it's leaving work on time or ensuring you end your evening work at a particular time so that you can attend to other priorities. Maybe it's as simple as leaving your phone on the counter once you get home from work so that you can be present with your family.

Walk through your day in your mind and start reflecting on the areas where your boundaries may have been stretched in unhealthy ways. Remember, your priorities are not defined by your words. Your priorities are defined by your actions.

> **Your priorities are not defined by your words. Your priorities are defined by your actions.**

Your Daily Habits = Your Future's Blueprint

Author and podcaster Scott Clary shared a story about one of his weekly meetings with his mentorship group, during which a fellow entrepreneur began to share his "dream life." The man discussed his vision board, full of time freedom, deep connection, and future financial prosperity. After he finished, Clary looked at him and asked, "But how's your Tuesday looking?" The silence was telling (Clary, 2025).

For most of us, it is easy to envision our "ideal life." At the same time, it's equally as easy to lose sight of the day we are currently living and the opportunity it presents. But our growth is not made up of highlight-reel moments. Instead, it comes from ordinary Tuesdays, lived with intentionality. This means that your *average day* is your *actual life*. Because of this, the value of your daily habits is more crucial than you may realize.

According to researchers at Duke University, habits account for approximately 40 percent of our behaviors on any given day–for better or worse (Neal et al., 2006). In other words, your life is built in 24-hour blocks, not in 5-year leaps. Our daily decisions, consistent execution, and "little bits of better" make all the difference in our long-term trajectory. As my friend and founder of *The Habit Lab*, Jenna Zint, says, "Your life is shaped by your habits, not just by your hopes" (Zint, n.d.).

So, how do you establish healthy habits in your life and consistently implement them each day? Willpower alone will not get you there. As you explore the five principles for habit building below, remember that habits are a marathon, not a sprint. Longevity, not intensity, is the ultimate goal.

ACT WITH DISCIPLINE AND CONSISTENCY

1. Anchor New Habits in Consistent Routines
Connect new habits to something you already do daily. For example, if you want to start journaling, do it right after making your cup of coffee in the morning. This will make it simpler to remember and integrate into your life.

2. Reduce Friction
The easier you make the habit to do, the less willpower you'll need to rely on to succeed. An example would be putting your alarm clock on the other side of the room so you no longer have the option of staying in bed and hitting the snooze button.

3. Start Small and Build Momentum
Focus on small, achievable steps rather than overwhelming goals. If you want to feel more connected with those you lead, focus on one or two people daily. Make the most of small interactions by asking questions about their lives or giving them a word of encouragement. Success

breeds confidence, as it builds trust in yourself that you are showing up like you told yourself you would.

4. Create Systems, Not Just Goals

Your goals set your direction, but your systems will create lasting change. Instead of saying, "I want to pursue my personal growth," create a system such as reading (perhaps *The Growth-Minded Leader*) for 15 minutes before bed each night. The key is to make the process *automatic*.

5. Track Your Progress and Stay Accountable

Use a habit tracker, accountability partner, or journal to measure your consistency. Visually seeing progress reinforces the habit, and having someone to check in with increases follow-through.

As Jim Rohn, author of *Take Charge of Your Life* (Rohn, 2024), suggests, "Success is a few small disciplines, practiced every day; while failure is simply a few small failures, repeated every day" (Rohn, 2018). When you commit to the *right* habits, you're not just changing your routine. You are *transforming your life* and the leader you are becoming, one day at a time.

The Discipline Difference

Discipline and consistency are not fleeting traits or occasional bursts of effort. They are the steady undercurrent of your growth. It will propel you from who you are today to the person you envision six months, a year, or even five years from now. Living a disciplined life is not easy, but it is deeply rewarding because it aligns your behaviors with your long-term vision.

Discipline and consistency form the rhythm that produces fruit not just in moments, but over a lifetime. While the world celebrates shortcuts and instant gratification, your transformation is built one

ACT WITH DISCIPLINE AND CONSISTENCY

decision at a time—especially when no one's clapping, watching, or rewarding your effort.

As you close this chapter, take time to evaluate what you're choosing each day. What habits are you building? What distractions are you eliminating? What priorities are you protecting—and what pain are you willing to endure to protect them? Show up every day, even when you don't feel like it. Stack your wins with consistency, and be deliberate in the small things. They are the ones that shape your character and lead to lasting breakthroughs. And remember: your growth compounds on persistence, not perfection.

LEADERSHIP IN ACTION: DISCIPLINE AND CONSISTENCY

We are what we repeatedly do. As a leader, your success—and your team's success—relies on the disciplined, consistent actions you take every day. Consistency fosters trust and stability within your team. When people know what to expect from you, it creates a sense of security that enables them to perform at their best.

This consistency can take many forms—being present and visible in your organization, holding regular one-on-one check-ins, following through on your commitments, or modeling the work ethic and values you expect from others. If you seek a culture of discipline and perseverance, it must start with you. Your team will take cues from how you show up—whether you're reliable and steady or unpredictable and inconsistent.

Your Pursuit of Growth:

1. Consistency is a catalyst for growth. Therefore, regular, dedicated actions over time compound into tangible progress. Spend time with your team and objectively assess the level of commitment and intentional action devoted to the specific goals you have set. Are there gaps or inefficiencies that have slowed progress or compromised your team's focus? If so, collaborate with your team to recalibrate and chart a plan to move forward. Ensure there is collective accountability to ensure that time, energy, and resources are being allocated with the consistency needed to see results. As the old saying goes, a farmer cannot expect to reap a harvest where he has not sown seeds.

ACT WITH DISCIPLINE AND CONSISTENCY

2. Identify and address gaps in your own consistency. Reflect on any areas where you have been inconsistent or lacked self-discipline. Have you set expectations but failed to uphold them? Have you been hit-or-miss in your presence, providing feedback, or following through? Identify one key habit to improve and commit to reinforcing it daily.

CHAPTER SEVEN

Reframe Your Mindset

THE "UNCHARTED" FRAMEWORK
9 KEYS FOR PURSUING YOUR POTENTIAL IN LEADERSHIP AND LIFE

U	UNDERSTAND YOUR LIMITING BELIEFS
N	NAVIGATE WITH VISION AND PURPOSE
C	CHOOSE TO TAKE OWNERSHIP
H	HARNESS RESILIENCE
A	ACT WITH DISCIPLINE AND CONSISTENCY
R	REFRAME YOUR MINDSET
T	TRANSFORM FAILURE INTO OPPORTUNITIES
E	EMBRACE COMMUNITY AND ACCOUNTABILITY
D	DARE TO CLIMB

THE GROWTH-MINDED LEADER

Duke Women's Basketball coach Kara Lawson has succeeded in nearly every athletic capacity imaginable. She boasts an All-American status at Tennessee, an Olympic gold medal, a WNBA championship, and was the first female NBA assistant coach, to name a few. But beneath all the accolades and shiny medals is a mentality forged and developed through persevering through trials and challenges from an early age.

From childhood pressures to fractured family relationships, Lawson faced a decision in her teen years: to shift her perspective and focus on her goals or let her difficulties define her. So, with a passion for growing to her fullest potential, Lawson became just as intentional in training her mindset as her basketball skills. As a result, years later and leading a team of her own, Lawson understood the value of developing her players' resilience and mental fortitude that would serve them long after their athletic years. In a 2022 speech that Lawson gave to her Duke Women's Basketball team, she unknowingly coined the phrase, "Handle hard better". According to Lawson:

> *In life, we all wait for things to get easier. But it will never get easier. What happens is you handle hard better. So, make yourself a person that handles hard well* (Duke Women's Basketball, 2022).

As the video went viral, "Handle hard better" resonated with teachers, CEOs, military personnel, and even cancer patients. During her speech to her team, Lawson went on to say,

> That's a mental shift that has to occur in each of you. Make yourself a person that handles hard well. Not someone that is waiting for the easy. Because if you have a meaningful pursuit in life, it will never be easy. If you are waiting for things to get easy, it's never going to happen. So, then what happens? "Oh, it's so hard. Oh, I can't do it. Oh, it's easy for other people." It's not. It's hard. So

become a person who handles hard better.

This perspective shifts the focus from wishing for "easy" to building the capacity and mindset to face adversity. Whether it is a tough season in your leadership, relationships, or personal life, the key is mastering your response to difficulties, even when you would rather search for the smoother path.

The More Pain You Expect, the More Pain You Feel

Have you ever gone to the doctor's office to get a shot and begin to feel your heart racing as you anticipate the pain you are about to feel? Have your palms started to sweat as you brace yourself for what's about to transpire, based on your expectation of discomfort? A new brain imaging study at the University of Colorado Boulder found that pain can be a self-fulfilling prophecy. In other words, *the more pain you expect, the more pain you feel.*

Research has shown that a feedback loop exists between expectation and discomfort. The more pain and discomfort you expect, the stronger your brain responds to the discomfort. The stronger your brain responds, the more pain you experience as a result (Marshall, 2018).

As a result of the research, neuroscientist Tor Wager has found that our expectations and mindset can influence everything from how we perform on a test, to how we push through physical demands, to how we respond to medication. The worse we think something will be, the more we activate the part of the brain designed to combat threat or fear, resulting in avoidance, timidity, and retreat.

Studies in the field of neuroscience confirm time and time again that our mind is our most powerful muscle. As we face the ups and downs of life, our mindset will determine if we limp through it with bruises and blame, or if we run through it with grit and determination.

Reflect on the areas of your life that you *expect* to be uncomfortable. What stories could you be telling yourself that are different from the reality of the situation? Too many people avoid the resilience required to push toward their potential, not because of the actual discomfort, but because of their *expectation* of it.

Your Mindset ROI

Your thoughts have a return on investment (ROI). As Roman Emperor Marcus Aurelius said, "The happiness of your life is determined by the quality of your thoughts" (Aurelius, 2019). In other words, your thoughts and perspective are the foundation upon which your reality is built. If you focus on gratitude, inspiration, and breakthroughs, your perspective and actions in life will follow. On the other hand, if you allow negative, defeating, or self-limiting thoughts to take the reins in your mind, you will find yourself stuck in a cycle of frustration and lack.

This begs an important question: what has a more significant impact on your life, more positive thinking or less negative thinking? Where do you get the most mileage? Dr. Price Pritchett, author of *You* (Pritchett & Pritchett, 1994) tackled this question, noting that research has shown that less negative thinking has a more significant impact on your life. Positive thinking is undoubtedly critical, but the ROI happens when you stop perseverating on those negative thought patterns.

The Dartmouth Experiment

Our mindsets are shaped through not only our circumstances but also our *perceptions* of our circumstances. This fine line between perception and reality can become a slippery slope, especially when we live from a powerless perspective that believes our external circumstances have more control over our growth and future than our own actions do. Chapter two (limiting beliefs) focused on the shackles of living with a victim mentality. Although not many would want to admit such a thing, this subtle mindset is not only a thief to our growth, but also alters how we show up in nearly every facet of our lives - from our leadership to our personal relationships.

In 1980, Dartmouth psychologist Robert Kleck conducted an experiment with a group of undergraduate students (Kleck & Strenta, 1980). The students were split into two groups, and one group was told they would have a large, visible scar painted on their faces by a makeup artist before a series of interviews. After the makeup was applied, they were shown their new "scar" in the mirror.

What the students did not know, however, is that before the interviews, the makeup artists removed the scar without them realizing it. They looked completely normal for their interviews. The results were intriguing. The students who believed they had a scar reported that the interviewers treated them differently. They felt judged, powerless, and disadvantaged in their interview based on their appearance. However, the participants without the supposed scar had no such feelings.

The takeaway? Our beliefs and mindsets change the way we view the world around us. When we believe that our struggles result from external things beyond our control, like our past, other people's actions, or outside influences, it's much harder to lead ourselves and focus on our own actions. We convince ourselves that we are stuck and that there's nothing we can do about it, which is a dangerous place to be. Many times, however, our *own mindset* is what holds us back.

PAUSE AND REFLECT:

1. *Where do you feel powerless? Where do you feel stuck and like you cannot break through because of external circumstances "bigger" than you?*

Get in Your Tree Stand

Of all my hobbies, whitetail deer hunting tops the list. The solitude of the forest, the year-long strategizing, and the physical work required for success check all the boxes for me. Additionally, as a father with three sons, it is something we love to do together. A few years ago, I decided to move a tree stand with my son, Elijah. At 18 feet in length and weighing 75 pounds, relocating a stand to a new tree in the forest can be an arduous task. However, after scouting the area, I found an optimal spot and told Elijah my plan.

Elijah looked around at the new location, paused, and said, "This spot is the worst! You can't see anything! There are bushes all around us."

I smiled and replied, "Trust me, son. This is the spot we were looking for."

Over the next thirty minutes, I proceeded to get the stand to its new location and leaned it against the tree. As I balanced myself nearly twenty feet off the ground while ratchet-strapping the stand into place, I heard Elijah call up from below. With annoyance in his voice, he shouted, "This isn't going to work!" I simply smiled and finished securing the stand.

Once completed, I looked at Elijah and said, "Hey son, do you want to be the first one to climb into the stand?" Excited, he ascended the ladder, step by step. Once he reached the top, he turned around and settled himself on the seat. He looked side to side as he scanned the forest, and the first words out of his mouth were, "Dad, you can see everything!"

The exact plot of land from a different vantage point gives proper perspective. One perspective sees the land as full of obstacles and barriers to our ultimate goal. From a higher perspective, however, the same land is primed for success.

Consider situations like this one in your life and your leadership. It's easy to get clouded by our emotions or caught in the "bushes" at the ground-level view. Sometimes, we need to climb in our tree stand, get out of the heat of the moment or our gut-level reactions, and look at our situation from a different point of view. Your perspective directly impacts your mindset, and your mindset directly impacts your growth.

Fixed vs. Growth Mindset

Your mindset serves in many ways as the foundation you build your life on—for better or for worse. In fact, the success of applying many of the principles in this book comes down to the mindset you are willing to cultivate, regardless of the season you are in or obstacles you encounter. Mindset separates those who climb higher from those who retreat down the mountain.

Stanford psychologist Carol Dweck coined the terms *fixed mindset* and *growth mindset* to describe people's underlying beliefs about their intelligence and ability (Dweck, 1999). In her book, *Mindset* (Dweck, 2017), she differentiated between the two mindsets in the following ways:

> **Fixed Mindset:** A person with a fixed mindset assumes that human qualities, such as intelligence, character, and ability are relatively stable and cannot be changed in any meaningful way. They were either born *with it* or they were born *without it*.

> **Growth Mindset:** A person with a growth mindset believes that human qualities are malleable and can improve with *effort*. Therefore, challenges, obstacles, and even failure are natural parts of learning and personal growth. They believe their growth is a *work in progress*.

The chart below visually compares what a fixed and a growth mindset may look like in our lives. Do any of these resonate with you?

GROWTH MINDSET	FIXED MINDSET
Embraces challenges	Avoids challenges
Views effort as a path to mastery	Views effort as fruitless
Learns from feedback	Ignores feedback
Inspired by others' success	Threatened by others' success
Perseveres in the face of setbacks	Gives up easily
Views failure as an opportunity for growth	Sees failure as proof of incompetence
Believes abilities can be developed	Believes abilities are fixed traits
Seeks learning and improvement	Sticks to comfort zone
Embraces change	Resists change
Leans into the unknown	Fears the unknown

People with a fixed mindset become easily frustrated by the learning curve of life, while those with a growth mindset accept the strain of the upward climb, embrace the struggle, and are patient with themselves when they make mistakes (Cury et al., 2006). If you tend to fall in the first category, the good news is that your mindset can change with self-awareness, intentionality, and consistency.

As an elementary principal in the field of education, one of my greatest priorities is to develop the character, self-belief, and mindset of every student who walks through our doors. Our students will inevitably grow academically during their time in our school, but my ultimate desire is for them to grow into young men and women who believe deep down that they have what it takes, while running toward the challenges they face in life with character and integrity. As a result, we are intentional as staff in fostering a culture in our school where the language of having a growth mindset appears throughout our hallways, in our classrooms, and during our interactions with students.

To reinforce our students' growth mindset, we often use Dweck's "Power of Yet" concept by pointing out "not yet" moments. For example, a "not yet" moment occurs when students struggle with a concept, perform poorly on an assessment, or encounter difficulties or barriers in their learning. In practicality, the power of "Yet" looks like:

I can't do this……………………………yet.
This doesn't work………………………yet.
I'm not good at this…………………yet.
I don't understand this……………yet.
This doesn't make sense……yet.

PAUSE AND REFLECT:

1. *Apply this to your own life. What areas of your life or leadership do you find yourself with a fixed mindset, saying things like, "I can't do this" or "I am not good at this?"*

2. *How can you reframe your perspective toward those situations to cultivate a growth mindset?*

A key catalyst to your growth is to become teachable–in every moment and situation. However, few teachable moments appear on a silver platter. Most occur in life's proverbial blood, sweat, and tears. Often the moments in which you would rather retreat down the mountain are the moments when the most noteworthy victories await you. Next time you feel like hanging your head, throwing in the towel, or partnering with defeat, just tell yourself: *I haven't figured this thing out… yet.*

Grit

University of Pennsylvania psychologist and author Angela Duckworth's concept on grit has reshaped how we understand the pursuit of growth and success in our lives (Duckworth, 2016). Duckworth's groundbreaking research defined "grit" as, "The passion and perseverance for very long-term goals. Grit is having stamina. Grit is sticking with your future, day in, day out, not just for the week. Not just for the month. But for years. And working really hard to make that future a reality."

Some other words that make up the attributes of grit are:

Courage	*Bravery*	*Backbone*	*Fortitude*
Resolve	*Determination*	*Endurance*	*Tenacity*
Strength of Will	*Guts*	*Perseverance*	*Mental Stamina*

Smooth Seas Do Not Build Skillful Sailors

The attributes of grit listed above are words that may spark a fire inside you and make you want to sit up a little straighter when you read them. They are the types of traits that all of us aspire to embody in our lives. The catch is, that demonstrating them requires us to embrace the situations that necessitate them.

For example, to embody courage, we must face circumstances that are fearful for us. To live with determination and tenacity, we must encounter scenarios that test our will, endurance, and resolve. And to develop mental toughness requires times in our lives when we must battle our inner voices that would talk us into quitting and settling for less. Grit grows in the *process* of growth. It is forged in the fire. As Franklin Roosevelt once said during his "Fireside Chat" radio broadcast in 1938, "Smooth seas do not build skillful sailors" (Roosevelt, 1938).

> Your life is not defined by the discomfort you try to avoid. It is defined by who you become through embracing the challenges along the way.

William Wallace

In the 1996 movie *Braveheart* (Gibson, 1995), Scottish warrior William Wallace led his countrymen in a rebellion to free his homeland from the tyranny of King Edward I of England, exemplifying grit in its purest form. In the film, Wallace was driven by an unwavering passion and determination to free his people under the brutal rule of England. Throughout his journey and the seemingly impossible feat of taking back the land that was rightfully theirs, Wallace endured heartache, betrayal, brutal battles, and personal sacrifices. However, his passion and commitment never wavered.

His vision for freedom amidst insurmountable odds fueled his pursuit. As he continued to fight, he began building momentum by inspiring others to join the cause. Wallace's perseverance mirrors two of the key components of grit: *sustained effort* and *resilience in the face of adversity*.

William Wallace's legacy reminds us that grit is more than just showing up for the fight, it's about staying committed even when the odds feel stacked against us. Life's most meaningful pursuits require a mindset marked by endurance and the belief that any obstacle can be overcome. As Wallace famously proclaimed on a hillside full of courageous countrymen preparing for battle, "Every man dies. But not every man really lives."

Grit is not something we are simply born with. It is built through pursuing our purpose with passion and perseverance, even when the inner battle rages around us.

Trusting the Process

One day, at a table full of people, a pastor asked an older farmer who was decked out in bib overalls to say grace for the morning breakfast. "Lord, I hate buttermilk," the farmer began. The visiting pastor opened one eye to glance at the farmer and wondered where this was going.

The farmer loudly proclaimed, "Lord, I hate lard!" Now, the pastor was growing concerned. Without missing a beat, the farmer continued, "And Lord, you know I don't care much for raw white flour." The pastor once again opened an eye to peek around the room and saw that he wasn't the only one feeling uncomfortable.

The farmer continued, "But Lord, when you mix them all together and bake them, I do love warm fresh biscuits. So Lord, when things get hard, when we don't understand what you're saying to us, help us to just relax and wait until you are done mixing. It will probably be even better than biscuits. Amen" (Dykes, 2017).

Everything in your life can have a purpose if you allow it to. Every season, every unknown, and every interaction. But the thing about life is that we only see in part. We react to the pain that we feel, often rationalizing what is in front of us based on our experience of the present moment. To grow, however, we have to be able to see the process, or the *long game*.

Reflect on the relationships in your life. There may be some people who feel like sandpaper to your skin. People who are challenging to have conversations with or test your patience. Instead of searching for the "fault" inside them, ask yourself what you may be lacking that needs to be *refined*. Perhaps it is empathy, patience, or even forgiveness.

Reflect on the trajectory of your career. There may be some seasons in your life that feel like a grind. Some projects or initiatives may test your fortitude and seem like another revolution on the never-ending hamster wheel. There may be steppingstones that take longer to ascend than you anticipated. Instead of growing impatient or disgruntled, ask yourself what areas can be developed in this season to *prepare you for the next*.

Reflect on the journey of your health. Perhaps it's the mundane ritual of working out, each exercise feeling like the movie, *Groundhog's Day* (Ramis, 1993). Maybe, it's the discipline of avoiding the comfort foods that continually entice you throughout the day or when you feel stressed. Or perhaps, it's the process of meal prepping instead of making the quick pit stop at your local convenience store. Rather than focusing on what you would rather eat, focus on your overall vision for your health and the longevity that will follow.

Whatever areas of your life wear on you, remind yourself of the value of the process. Most of the time, you won't notice a physical difference after one workout. However, if you continue stacking days, your workouts will create a different version of you. You won't always feel better after leaning into a challenging relationship with patience and empathy, but after a while, you will notice your heart begin to soften and see the gold inside of others.

These processes in our lives also often reveal our shortcomings. They indicate areas in our lives such as lies, doubts, and gaps in our armor that we wouldn't have known otherwise. These are the areas where we can grow. So, make the conscious effort to see the big picture amidst everyday life. Growth rarely happens in singular moments, but instead by trusting the process, day in and day out.

> Everything in your life can have a purpose if you allow it to.

What You Think, You Become

Your mindset shapes not only how you see the world, but also how you see yourself. In other words, *you are what you think*. Whether you believe you can or believe you can't—you're right. Your mindset is more than a buzzword you hear psychologists use or a catchy phrase on social media. It's the internal filter through which you interpret every experience. Your mindset is either *feeding you* or *depleting you* each day.

As this chapter comes to a close, take an honest assessment of your perspectives. Ask yourself: *Is your inner dialogue nurturing your growth, or is it filling you with doubt, shame, and fear?* If you find your thoughts stealing from your growth, choose one or two areas to focus on where you've been holding yourself back. Become keenly aware of your reactions, your self-talk, and your responses to situations that arise over the coming weeks. Developing self-awareness will allow you to red flag the areas of your mindset that are fixed, rather than growth oriented.

As you build this foundation, the next chapter will tackle one of the most critical crossroads to your growth—failure. You have two options when encountering failure—it can either *define* you or it can *refine* you. With a growth mindset, however, every obstacle in your life becomes an invitation for your forward progress.

LEADERSHIP IN ACTION: MINDSET

Your mindset as a leader determines how you navigate difficult situations, inspire others, and pursue your team's goals. Leaders with a fixed mindset see obstacles as limitations—ultimately putting a lid on their own potential and that of their team. On the other hand, leaders with a growth mindset embrace challenges, seek opportunities to improve, and instill a belief in continuous learning within their teams.

Your mindset sets the tone for your organization. If you view setbacks as learning experiences and approach problems with curiosity rather than frustration, your team will follow suit. If you react with resistance or negativity, that mindset will also ripple through your organization.

For example, when a project or initiative does not go as planned, a fixed mindset leader might say, "This didn't work. Maybe we aren't capable of pulling this off." In contrast, a growth-minded leader would ask, "What information can we gather from this? How can we adjust and improve moving forward?" The latter responses display a perspective that sees the mountain as an invitation, rather than a threat.

Your Pursuit of Growth:

1. Reframe challenges as opportunities. Look at the complicated scenario you are facing as a chance to expand your abilities, rather than a hazard to avoid. Do not just look at it as a sign of weakness, but rather an invitation to develop the strengths of your leadership.

2. Embed a growth mindset in your team's language. Use and reinforce phrases like "We're not there yet" instead of "We can't do this." The language you use on a consistent basis will shape how your team views and responds accordingly to circumstances.

CHAPTER EIGHT

Transform Failure Into Opportunities

THE "UNCHARTED" FRAMEWORK
9 KEYS FOR PURSUING YOUR POTENTIAL IN LEADERSHIP AND LIFE

U	UNDERSTAND YOUR LIMITING BELIEFS
N	NAVIGATE WITH VISION AND PURPOSE
C	CHOOSE TO TAKE OWNERSHIP
H	HARNESS RESILIENCE
A	ACT WITH DISCIPLINE AND CONSISTENCY
R	REFRAME YOUR MINDSET
T	**TRANSFORM FAILURE INTO OPPORTUNITIES**
E	EMBRACE COMMUNITY AND ACCOUNTABILITY
D	DARE TO CLIMB

THE GROWTH-MINDED LEADER

In 1991, a lanky fourteen-year-old tried out for his high school junior varsity football team in San Mateo, California. After discovering he was not good enough to start for the previously 0-8 team, he spent his first season as the backup quarterback. After the starter quit the following year, he finally got his chance to prove himself.

Despite the obstacles in front of him, the next two years were filled with developing a mindset of resilience and discipline, just as much as it was developing arm strength and passing accuracy. He honed his skills and began marketing himself to scouts, eventually catching the eye of the University of Michigan, who offered him a spot on the team. However, becoming a Wolverine did not mean he would immediately find success on the field, nor would it be without its own trials.

The teenager joined the collegiate program as the seventh quarterback on the depth chart. Three long years later, his patience and determination paid off, earning him the opportunity to start as a junior. Over the next two years, he continued to push himself mentally and physically, with a dream of one day playing in the NFL.

However, during his final days of college, his coach at Michigan only received one phone call from an interested NFL scout. Even so, that did not deter the underrated and underestimated kid from California from taking a chance at entering the scouting combine. At the 2000 NFL combine, his draft report did not mince any words. It stated numerous criticisms such as: *poor build, skinny, lacks mobility, doesn't throw a tight spiral, lacks a strong arm, gets knocked down easily*, and more (The Strive, n.d.).

What the scouts could not measure, however, was his mindset, grit, and vision to pursue his goals. During the 2000 NFL Draft, 198 players were chosen ahead of him. When the New England Patriots finally called his name in the sixth round, he was an afterthought by nearly every team in the league. Who was the player selected as the 199th pick in the draft? Tom Brady. Brady went on to win an NFL record of seven Super Bowls over his storied, 23-year career. Widely regarded

TRANSFORM FAILURE INTO OPPORTUNITIES

as the greatest quarterback of all time, his accolades and records are unmatched by any player in NFL history.

What was the key to his success? His perspective on failure and the obstacles that stood in the way of who he knew he could be. Brady refused to let roadblocks define him and viewed the word "underdog" as an opportunity. He worked tirelessly, showed up early, stayed late, and committed himself to the daily grind of improvement. He simply refused to let his present circumstances hold him back. As a speaker at the 2023 10x Growth Conference, after he retired from football, Brady shared his perspective on failure:

> *There will come opportunities in life. When they're presented to you, in front of you. It's just a matter of whether you're prepared to take advantage of the opportunity.*
>
> *But, you've got to develop that resilience within you. Life is not about how much you succeed. It's about what happens when you fail. If you said, 'Tom, what have been the greatest wins?' Ah, the wins… let's talk about the losses. Those are the ones that really made me who I am.*
>
> *As you go through life, things happen that you don't want to happen. Whether you lose a game, whether things don't go well at work, or something with your child. There's a lot of things that come up in our personal and professional lives that just don't go the way we want.*
>
> *So how do you deal with it? You deal with it with class and integrity and courage and resilience. Life will be what you make of it.* (Brady, 2024)

Brady's story is a reminder that failure is not final and that the lessons you are willing to learn in your

> **The lessons you are willing to learn in your moments of struggle hold the key to opening the next door in your life.**

moments of struggle might just hold the key to open the next door in your life.

The Lesson Under the Rock

In Ryan Holiday's book, *The Obstacle is the Way* (Holiday, 2015), he shares an old story about a king whose people had grown complacent and entitled. Frustrated by their lack of grit and determination, he wanted to teach them a lesson. So, he created a plan. He placed a large boulder on the main road, blocking entry to the city. Then, he hid nearby to observe how the people would respond.

One by one, travelers approached the obstruction. The king grew disheartened as he watched person after person evaluate the boulder and turn away. At best, some would feebly attempt for a moment to move it, but they quickly gave up. Many complained and criticized the king for the inconvenience and not keeping the road clear, yet no one attempted to move it.

Days passed until a lone peasant finally traveled toward town and approached the boulder. After examining the rock, he decided to act instead of turning back. He explored the nearby forest until he found some branches that were sturdy enough to create a lever. Resolute to move the large stone, he worked until the boulder finally budged and shifted out of the way. To the peasant's surprise, he looked down where the rock once was and found a purse of gold coins and a note from the king, which stated:

> *The obstacle in the path becomes the path.*
> *Never forget, within every obstacle is an opportunity to improve our condition.*

Each one of us has boulders in our lives. They may be mental, physical, relational, professional, or personal. But just as in the story of the king and the boulder, the true obstacle is rarely an external barrier. The inner battle must be won first to rise above, push through, and overcome. As a result, the perspective with which we view our challenges determines whether we find the gold under the boulder.

Those on the journey who viewed the boulder as an inconvenience and blamed the king for their situation had already lost the battle in their minds before ever attempting to move it. Along with losing out on the opportunity to prevail, they also missed the reward under the stone. It could be said that the real boulder was their *attitude* and *perspective*, rather than a simple rock in the way.

PAUSE AND REFLECT:

1. *What is the external boulder currently in your path? It may be physical resources for your vision or even the environment you have created due to complacency or lack of discipline.*

2. *Next, look inward and ask yourself: What internal boulder needs rolled away first? Is it your perspective? Is it your fear of failure? Or even your lack of resolve, which results in giving up too soon?*

The answer to this second question is your starting point. It is the key to determining whether you view your struggle as an opportunity to overcome or a threat to avoid. One will sustain you through the process and the other will keep you stuck and focused on the stone in your way.

Navigating Setbacks in Leadership and Life

It is unlikely that you have encountered a physical rock in your path anytime recently, but chances are you have experienced many other kinds of setbacks in your life and leadership. Although some can feel monumental, most are a natural part of "doing life." You might even be feeling the weight of something right now, as you read this book. Something such as:

- A leadership decision that backfired, like hiring the wrong person, mishandling an interaction with an employee, or implementing a strategy that didn't work.
- Missing out on an opportunity in your life that could have led to breakthrough, which has now left you feeling disheartened and unsure of what to do next.
- A conflict at work which has impacted your team's culture and morale, now resulting in dysfunction among team members.
- A personal setback such as health issues, challenging family dynamics, or financial burdens that weigh on you both physically and emotionally.
- Battling burnout due to overcommitting and overextending yourself in areas of your life, resulting in strife or disconnection at home or work.
- Loss of momentum toward your goals due to lack of discipline or a busy season, leading to feelings of falling behind or guilt.

Whatever you encounter or may be feeling, there is always opportunity in the midst. As stated previously, the greatest challenges you face in life are not necessarily found in your circumstances—they are within yourself. Winning the battle starts in your mind and acknowledging that although you may not have full control over the outcome of the *external* situation, you *do* have one hundred percent control of your *internal* world. Your inner response to failure and resistance will determine how you view and respond to whatever is happening around you. Like Zig Ziglar once said, "Your attitude determines your altitude" (Ziglar, 2013).

> The greatest challenges you face in life are not necessarily found in your circumstances—they are within yourself.

What is Your Default?

While navigating failure and setbacks, forward momentum begins when you are willing to honestly assess what fears, lies, and limiting beliefs are competing for your focus. For example, early in my leadership career, I would feel embarrassed and subconsciously withdraw when I would make a mistake or mishandle a situation. I associated making a mistake or "failing" with the inner voice of, *I am a failure.* I would tell myself the story that people no longer believed in me and I felt very self-conscious. This lie held me captive and clouded my view forward. It hindered my confidence, and I am sure it showed.

However, after a mentor encouraged me to pinpoint and put language to what I was truly feeling, I was able to identify the lie that I was believing and begin renewing my mind to the truth that, *Just because I made a mistake, doesn't mean I am a mistake.*

Leading is not for the faint of heart, and not every decision will be perfect. But often our inner dialogue can get in the way of having the resilience to keep our heads up high and move forward with confidence, humility, and resolve to get back in the saddle and try again. Think about your own life. Can you think of default mindsets you slip into when the going gets tough?

- Maybe it's the feeling of rejection in a relationship. As a result of your pain, you take your foot off the gas pedal and keep the

other person at arm's length, rather than being in charge of your own heart and moving toward them.
- Maybe, you have overextended yourself to the point where you feel burned out and exhausted. Now, you start believing the lie that giving of yourself and serving others will only drain you, so you start becoming bitter and disappointed toward others.
- Or, you took a risk on a business endeavor that did not pan out, and now you are struggling with fear to take a leap again.

Oftentimes the stories we tell ourselves are a mixture of the reality of the situation and our subconscious fears. Once you are willing to identify and confront the fear, you then have a much clearer path forward. Just as mold only grows in the dark, until your fears or limiting beliefs are exposed, they will continue reinforcing a message in your life that is bound to keep you captive.

> **PAUSE AND REFLECT:**
>
> 1. *Which of these scenarios resonates with you? What are the areas in your life where you experience fear of failure, rather than courage and confidence?*

4 Steps to Growing Through Failure and Setbacks

Failure and setbacks are inevitable, but what you do afterward makes all the difference. When setbacks occur, it's easy to feel disheartened and difficult to rise above them. That is where having a clear, actionable process comes in. Use the four steps below as a tool for those crossroads and turn failure into feedback for your next steps forward:

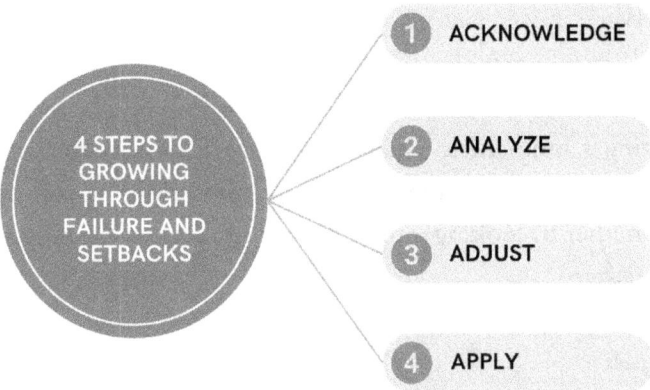

1. Acknowledge

Confront your setback head-on. Don't sugarcoat it, minimize it, or avoid the reality of what is happening. After all, you can't fix a problem you aren't willing to acknowledge. Accept responsibility, take ownership, then:

- *Process through your emotions (using the Emotion Wheel from Chapter 4).*
- *Ask yourself what went wrong.*
- *Determine your role in the outcome.*

Great leaders do not shift blame. Instead, they acknowledge the situation, take responsibility, and shift toward the solution.

2. Analyze

After establishing an objective view of the situation, take time to understand the root cause(s). Take your emotions out of the scenario, and turn into a scientist by evaluating and considering the following:

- *What were the contributing factors?*
- *What assumptions or decisions led to this result?*
- *Were there external factors beyond my control?*
- *Were there internal factors that clouded my approach or decision-making?*

Taking a moment to analyze and assess the situation objectively will allow you to make the appropriate corrections as you move forward, whether by looking more clearly at the data or cleaning up a relational misstep.

3. Adjust

After you have taken ownership and established the root causes, make the adjustments necessary to move ahead. Your target could be your strategy or even your mindset. Start by asking yourself:

- *What changes can I make to improve?*
- *How can I strengthen my skillset to avoid repeating this same mistake?*
- *Are there any gaps in my mindset that are stealing from my success?*

This is the pivot point that will reposition you towards your "True North," which requires self-awareness and follow-through.

4. Apply

Your application is where the rubber meets the road. It is time to put what you have learned into action. Determine:

- *What is the next actionable step I need to take?*
- *How will I measure progress and success moving forward?*
- *How can I build accountability into my process?*

TRANSFORM FAILURE INTO OPPORTUNITIES

Here is where the growth happens. How will you move forward with intentionality amid the hard things you would rather avoid? Remember, it is only *truly a failure* if you *quit*.

"Good."

Jocko Willink, author of *Extreme Ownership*, is no stranger to failure and setbacks. As a retired U.S. Navy SEAL Officer, Willink served as commander of Seal Team Three's Task Unit Bruiser, which became the most highly decorated Special Operations Unit of the Iraq War.

Battle-tested and passionate about leadership development, Willink returned from Iraq as Officer-in-Charge of leadership training for the next generation of SEAL leaders. After retiring from the Navy, Willink authored multiple best-selling books on leadership, living with discipline, and taking radical personal responsibility for every aspect of life.

On episode three of his podcast (Jocko Podcast, 2015), Willink shared a profound perspective on his approach to dealing with failures—not just on the battlefield, but in life:

> *"How do I deal with setbacks, failures, delays, defeats, or other disasters? I actually have a fairly simple way of dealing with these situations, summed up in one word: 'Good.'*
>
> *One of my direct subordinates, one of the guys who worked for me, he would call me up or pull me aside with some major problem or some issue that was going on, and he would say, "Boss, we've got this, that, or some other thing, and I would look at him and say, 'Good.'*
>
> *And finally, one day, he was telling me about some issue he was having, some problem, and he said, "I already know what you're going to say."*
>
> *And I said, "What am I going to say?"*

And he said, "You're going to say, 'Good.'"
"That's what you always say. When something is wrong or going bad, you always just look at me and say, 'Good.'"
And I said, "Well yeah. When things are going bad, there is going to be some good that is going to come from it.
Didn't get the new high-speed gear we wanted? Good.
Didn't get promoted? Good. More time to get better.
Mission got canceled? Good. We can focus on another one.
Didn't get funded? Didn't get the job you wanted? Got injured? Sprained your ankle? Got tapped out? Good.
Got beat? Good. You learned.
Unexpected problems? Good. We have the opportunity to figure out a solution.
That's it. When things are going bad, don't get all bummed out. Don't get startled. Don't get frustrated.
If you can say the word, 'Good,' guess what? It means you're still alive, it means you're still breathing. And if you're still breathing, that means you've still got some fight left in you.
So get up. Dust off. Reload. Recalibrate. Re-engage. Go out on the attack. Get after it."

This perspective from Willink is not some trite example of toxic positivity. It was forged behind enemy lines in the toughest battles and through the bleakest circumstances. There was no time to sulk and no time for self-pity. As a result, he led his teams, created a powerful culture among his men, and turned *barriers* into *bridges* for growth, success, and victory.

As Willink noted, a positive attitude alone will not solve your problems. But, neither will dwelling on your problems. Overcoming means accepting reality, focusing on the solution, taking action, and moving forward. When you do this as a leader, you create an ecosystem that helps build this same capacity in those you lead. It becomes the process by which your team approaches roadblocks and tackles the disappointments in front of them.

Built to Win

Contrary to how it may feel, failure and difficulty are not dead ends. They are merely a step in the process that will help equip you with the tools and resources you need to reach your potential. That is if you lean in and allow it to. You may not be leading a Special Operations Force in the Middle East, but you *are* leading your team and you *are* leading your family.

What response do you model at work when you hit a snag on a project or battle the underperformance of an initiative? What response do you model in your kitchen in front of your family when you encounter a difficulty that disrupts your plans or disheartens you? It all starts with doing the inner work *before* the battle comes knocking on your door.

Throughout this book and the UNCHARTED Framework, the focus has been on confronting the limiting beliefs that are in opposition to your progress, developing a laser-focused vision for your growth, taking ownership of whatever season you are in, and then developing the discipline, habits, and mindset necessary to face the resistance in front of you head-on.

The victories in your life start with your preparation before the storm comes, and are then won in the midst of the storm. When you build your life on solid ground with a mindset geared toward growth, the toughest seasons of your life and the hard things you would rather avoid are where your most substantial growth occurs.

Don't look to side-step your hard seasons. Don't work harder on seeking comfort than you do leaping the hurdles in your way. And don't be afraid of failure, as it is feedback for your life and fuel for the direction you are heading. As legendary actor Mickey Rooney once said, "You will always pass failure on the way to success" (Rooney, n.d.).

The Gift of Adversity

Failure is not the opposite of growth and success in your life. It's a crucial *part of it*. Whether you find yourself in the role of the underdog, like Tom Brady early in his career, standing face-to-face with an immovable obstacle, or confronting unexpected challenges that test your resolve, each situation is an invitation to develop your character and strengthen you for your next season.

In life, we're always navigating storms—either we're in the midst of one, emerging from one, or preparing for the next. Whatever place you find yourself in, your perspective makes all the difference. Everyone wants growth, but few are willing to endure the process it takes to get there. Picture this as the *growth gap*—the chasm between where you are and want to be. This gap is not to be feared, though. It must be embraced. Within it are the trials that equip, refine, and propel you toward becoming the person you desire to be.

The good news is, you don't have to navigate this gap alone. The most profound breakthroughs often happen in partnership with those who walk alongside you—offering support, wisdom, and a perspective that can both encourage and challenge you. In the next chapter, we'll explore the role of these relationships in fueling your growth and helping you reach your full potential.

LEADERSHIP IN ACTION: FAILURE AND SETBACKS

Failure is inevitable in leadership. It is not the opposite of success but a necessary part of it. How you respond to failure, however, makes all the difference. Growth-minded leaders view failure as fuel for their growth. They learn from it, make the needed adjustments, and move forward. When you are shaken by every difficulty or panic in every predicament, your team notices. Your team looks at you for strength and resolve, even when the bottom falls out.

Your response in moments of failure sets the standard for others to follow. If you react with frustration, fear, or avoidance, you model that your problem is bigger than your ability to solve it. Instead, openly acknowledge setbacks, diagnose what went wrong, and turn them into learning moments–bringing your team along for the journey. When something goes awry, such as a failed project, a misstep in execution, or a strategic miscalculation—be transparent about it. Some of the most galvanizing moments for teams and organizations have been amid adversity, where collective resolve ultimately triumphed over seemingly insurmountable odds.

Your Pursuit of Growth:

1. Normalize failure as part of the growth process. Share stories of your own failures and how they contributed to your development. Additionally, model for your team in real-time what it looks like to reframe your perspective and tackle situations as they occur.

2. Debrief failures with curiosity, not criticism. After a setback, facilitate open discussions with your team about what worked, what did not, and how to improve for the future. When people feel involved in finding the solution and that they have a voice around the table, they will be more likely to contribute and take ownership of the solution.

CHAPTER NINE

Embrace Community and Accountability

THE "UNCHARTED" FRAMEWORK
9 KEYS FOR PURSUING YOUR POTENTIAL IN LEADERSHIP AND LIFE

- **U** — UNDERSTAND YOUR LIMITING BELIEFS
- **N** — NAVIGATE WITH VISION AND PURPOSE
- **C** — CHOOSE TO TAKE OWNERSHIP
- **H** — HARNESS RESILIENCE
- **A** — ACT WITH DISCIPLINE AND CONSISTENCY
- **R** — REFRAME YOUR MINDSET
- **T** — TRANSFORM FAILURE INTO OPPORTUNITIES
- **E** — EMBRACE COMMUNITY AND ACCOUNTABILITY
- **D** — DARE TO CLIMB

In the high-stakes world of Formula 1 racing, the difference between victory and defeat is often determined by fractions of a second. While the driver may get the spotlight, every race is won (or lost) with the help of an elite pit crew working together in perfect unison. During a race, there are multiple pit stops that require both speed and precision as engineers and mechanics change tires, add fuel, make adjustments, and send the driver back on the track as quickly and efficiently as possible for the next leg of their race. This process requires communication, accountability, and trust at the highest level.

Even the strongest and most skilled drivers cannot win the race alone. The same can also be said of our lives. We need a community—a pit crew. These trusted relationships will provide us with the support and feedback to help us stay on track and in the race. These relationships in our lives help us navigate sharp turns, refuel when we are running on empty, and keep us accountable to operate at our highest level. Without them, we risk burning out or taking a wrong turn. As Robin Jones Gunn said, "If you want to go fast, go alone. If you want to go far, go together" (Gunn, 2009).

The Cornerstone

The first eight chapters of this book focus on doing the hard, personal work necessary for your growth. It has served as a call to advance toward your potential, even amid adversity, trials, or living outside your comfort zone. The message that has resonated throughout these pages is that you are in charge of your growth, and it is a choice you must make every single day.

Although growth is a personal choice, we are not created to run this race alone. We need *community*. We need trusted people to whom we give permission to give us feedback and hold us accountable. Although this requires humility and vulnerability at times, it is the only authentic, sustainable path forward.

EMBRACE COMMUNITY AND ACCOUNTABILITY

As human beings, we are hardwired for connection. Throughout human history, collaboration and relationships have been the key to survival, innovation, and growth. When we live in connection with others, they provide us perspective when we are stuck, encouragement when we are discouraged, and strength when we slow down or feel like giving up.

Your Support Team

In my book *Building Authenticity* (Cook & Nesloney, 2023), I discuss the value of developing a support system in your life. These are people that you trust, such as a close friend, a spouse, a mentor, a pastor, or a co-worker. They have your best interest in mind and genuinely want to see you win in life. They love you for who you are, not conditionally based on your successes or failures. They see you through the lens of your potential and use the relational access point into your life to speak honestly, candidly, and even share the things you may not want to hear. These people are a *gift* to your life and are integral to your growth.

So, who are those people in your circle? More importantly, have you permitted them to speak honestly into your life? Although each of us has those whom we trust, tapping into the real depth and incredible resources of those relationships requires a humble invitation on our end.

> Who have you given permission to speak into your life?

Some years ago, as I pursued growth in some areas of my life, specifically in my marriage, I was riding in my truck with one of my close friends and mentors. As I shared some pain points and areas where I felt stuck, he sat quietly and listened. As I finished, he smiled and replied, "Do you want me to tell you what you *want* to hear, or do you want me to tell you what you *need* to hear?"

It was in that moment that it clicked. I knew that if I truly wanted to grow, I did not need someone to simply agree and side with me. I needed someone to give me the necessary feedback for my growth and speak the truth into my life—even if it felt uncomfortable.

As my heart rate slowly elevated amid not knowing what would come next, I turned to him and said, "I want you to tell me what I need to hear." As he pointed out some areas where I was viewing the situation through the lens of unforgiveness and making assumptions based on my own hurts, I realized that there are things in my life that *I simply cannot see on my own*. I have blind spots that I am unaware of, yet others can see and help me navigate through. So, if I sincerely wanted to grow, I needed people with permission to share these things with me.

Reflect again on those people in your life that you trust. Have you offered them *permission* to share with you when they see you fading off course? More importantly, are you open to their feedback or do you lash out with defensiveness or out of embarrassment?

When you open your heart and are willing to receive feedback, it becomes like a cheat code for your trajectory. As a result, you can see situations more clearly and pinpoint areas that would otherwise continue to hold you back. Remember, your support team loves you for who you are, but they love you too much to let things steal from your life and rob you of your potential.

You may be overcommitting in an area of your life, leaving other facets to suffer as a byproduct. You may have personal goals that you pursue for a season but end up fading off time and time again. Or, it could be something as subtle as a tone of voice that you do not realize you use in meetings or certain situations. Whatever it may be, these *blind spots* can unknowingly drift you off course from your goals, negatively impacting you or even those you care about.

For these reasons, trusted relationships are valuable in your life. They know your heart and intentions and are willing to say, "I see this area in your life that is holding you back from who I know you intend to be. Would you be willing to take some time to reflect on this area?" All from a place of love and with your best interest in mind (Cook & Nesloney, 2023).

Accountability, Support, and Feedback– The Trifecta for Growth

Just as willpower alone is not enough to sustain you towards your goals, neither is climbing the mountain on your own. When it comes to your support system, as described above, think of accountability, support, and feedback as the trifecta that enables you to go further, faster, and more focused.

1. Accountability

Accountability is one of the most overlooked tools for personal growth, and it has been proven to increase the effectiveness of reaching your goals. In a study conducted by the American Society of Training and Development (ASTD), those who welcome accountability increase the likelihood of achieving their goals by 65%. Even more so, when coupled with regular check-ins with a specific person, that same success rate rises to a staggering 95% (Connors et al., 2015). When you have someone to whom you are consistently accountable, you are more likely to stay disciplined, focus on your vision for growth, and follow through in the areas you said you would.

2. Support

Layering a support system into your life is not only integral to your progress but also vital when it comes to the challenges and setbacks you encounter. Research published by the Journal of Applied Psychology noted that having a support system in life helps mitigate the negative effects of stressors and setbacks (Viswesvaran et al., 1999). When you feel supported and not alone in the storms of life, you are more likely to persevere, push through your difficulties, and maintain the perspective that will propel you through to the other side.

3. Feedback

Finally, feedback focuses on revealing your blind spots that others see when you do not. It is like the friend that lets you know when you have pepper between your teeth. Those people are a blessing, as they help bring awareness to the hidden things limiting you or unknowingly holding you back. Although many generally associate feedback with workplace performance, the actual gold is found on a personal level. This is because your personal growth impacts how you appear in every other area of your life. From helping identify patterns of negative thinking to your default responses to difficulties, those closest to you can give you honest information that, when openly received by you, can benefit everything from your leadership to your relationships.

> **Accountability and feedback are a gift to your life.**

The Isolation Trap

One of the most consequential traps that can hinder our growth is partnering with the lies of fear and shame that keep us from opening ourselves up to others. The message of fear says that by being vulnerable with others amid our struggles, they will judge us and view us differently. So, we stay hidden, fearful of transparency and allowing others into our lives. Shame, on the other hand, speaks straight to your identity. It says that you *are* your shortcomings and targets your self-worth.

These insecurities that often start in childhood can convince us that the risk of being vulnerable with others—even those who care about us—is simply too much. Living in isolation might feel "safe" at the time, but it comes at the cost of deep relationships, living in connection with others, and the resulting opportunities to grow.

The value of living in community with others cannot be overstated. Studies in behavioral psychology show that people are more likely to stay disciplined toward their goals and committed to the habits they are developing when they are a part of a group pursuing similar goals (Bryksina, 2024). However, this does not just mean New Year's resolutions such as going to the gym three times a week or cutting out carbohydrates.

For example, I want to be a father who is present with my children. I want to be a husband who loves and pursues my wife daily, fostering connection and modeling what it means to be a godly man to my family. Therefore, I have invested in relationships with other men in my life who are pursuing the same in *their* lives and homes. Over the past few years, I have met weekly on Zoom with a group of like-minded men, led by Jason Vallotton, founder of *BraveCo*.

We share our wins, lean on each other in our losses, and hold each other accountable. We encourage each other and hold each other to the standard we have set for our lives. We check in with one another, spend time processing our journeys, and welcome feedback from each other. This level of transparency and connectedness has been such a catalyst for growth in my own life. They are both a source of encouragement and also serve as guardrails to help keep me on course.

This aligns with the vital role of "community," as it pertains to identity-based habits that James Clear emphasizes in his book, *Atomic Habits* (Clear 2018). When we surround ourselves with people who embody similar behaviors we want to adopt and the same type of growth we desire, it creates a powerful social norm that encourages a more focused pursuit.

> **PAUSE AND REFLECT:**
>
> 1. Who are the people in your life who share a similar value system that you can invite to support you in your pursuit of growth and who you are becoming?
>
> 2. In what area(s) of your life can you partner with them as a source of accountability, support, and feedback for each other?

I remember sitting in a small living room at my youth leader's house as a teenager, and he would say to us, "Show me your friends, and I'll show you your future." Admittedly, however, as a 16-year-old, my future was not my focus. I was more concerned with playing my guitar, getting my driver's license, and spending time with my new girlfriend (now my wife). But looking back, those words could not have been more profound.

The company you keep either serves as the wind at your back or in your face. They either climb the mountain with you, encouraging you when your legs start to get shaky, or questioning why the sacrifice is even worth it in the first place. When you surround yourself with those who are committed to helping you win in life, you have the opportunity to lean on their strength when times get tough. Although your growth is always *your choice*, you can always go further when you have others climbing alongside you.

Iron Sharpens Iron

Self-awareness, personal discipline, and individual efforts are critical, but we are also meant to live connected with others. We are designed for relationships, and the connections we cultivate are an essential part of our growth. Just as iron sharpens iron, we need people who will push us to beyond our comfort zone, challenge us to face our toughest mountains, and hold us accountable to our vision. A life rooted in genuine community, accountability, and openness to feedback prevents us from justifying excuses and settling for mediocrity.

When we invite others to speak into our lives, we are forced to confront our blind spots and courageously change course when necessary. Let those you trust tell you what you need to hear, not just what you want to hear. Allow them to serve as the mirror that reflects both your strengths and your weaknesses. And just as they help to refine you, step into the same role for them. Let your life be an encouragement, infusing others with courage, hope, and belief in their potential. There is immense power in emboldening one another and rising together through the strength of shared accountability and mutual support.

LEADERSHIP IN ACTION: COMMUNITY AND ACCOUNTABILITY

Leadership can often feel like a lonely road. The higher you go, the fewer people there seem to be who truly understand the weight of your responsibilities. This results in many leaders falling into isolation, believing they must carry everything on their own. However, there is no substitute for connection and relationship with those you can rely on in the tough times—those who can support you, provide honest feedback, and even challenge you when you need it.

Who do you turn to when you face a challenging season in your leadership? Do you have trusted colleagues, mentors, or peers to lean on? Or do you try to figure it all out yourself? Growth-minded leaders actively welcome support from those they trust because they know their growth and success depend on it. No leader can thrive in a vacuum, as it is a recipe for stagnation and burnout.

Furthermore, community and accountability are also vital for the growth of your team. Healthy, high-performing teams thrive on trust, relationships, and open communication. This requires creating an environment where feedback is normalized, not feared. Your team should feel empowered to speak up when something is not working, offer solutions, and respectfully challenge each other (and you) to pursue excellence.

Some ways to foster this culture include implementing weekly check-ins, post-project debriefs, or open forums where your team can freely discuss challenges. When leaders model vulnerability by welcoming feedback on their own performance, it sends a powerful message—accountability is a key component of growth.

Your Pursuit of Growth:

1. Create a culture of open dialogue where feedback flows freely. The more people feel safe to share ideas, communicate concerns, or simply ask for support, the greater the level of trust developed. A connected culture is a powerful culture.
2. Invest in your own personal leadership development by joining an online leadership community or a mastermind group of like-minded leaders who can challenge your thinking, provide perspective, and hold you accountable for your growth.

CHAPTER TEN

Dare to Climb

THE "UNCHARTED" FRAMEWORK
9 KEYS FOR PURSUING YOUR POTENTIAL IN LEADERSHIP AND LIFE

U	UNDERSTAND YOUR LIMITING BELIEFS
N	NAVIGATE WITH VISION AND PURPOSE
C	CHOOSE TO TAKE OWNERSHIP
H	HARNESS RESILIENCE
A	ACT WITH DISCIPLINE AND CONSISTENCY
R	REFRAME YOUR MINDSET
T	TRANSFORM FAILURE INTO OPPORTUNITIES
E	EMBRACE COMMUNITY AND ACCOUNTABILITY
D	DARE TO CLIMB

There is no easy path up the mountain. As you stand at its base, the only path toward your growth requires something different from you, found only in the things you would likely rather avoid. Your progress up the incline and the mile markers you pass only occur through the ownership you take, the discipline you embody, the resilience you develop, and the failures you learn from. In this place, you will be refined with the character and mindset necessary to take your land and stake your claim on the mountains in your way.

As you near the end of this book, you have two options: You can choose the *discomfort of growth now* to have the life, marriage, relationships, and leadership that you want later, or you can choose *comfort now* and stay stuck in the same place, circling the same mountain over and over again. Reflect back to chapter three on vision and purpose, and ask yourself these questions once more:

- *What would be the cost of inaction in my life one year from now? Three years from now?*
- *What will be the cost of inaction regarding my relationships, health, or impact on my family?*

These are very real questions with very real ramifications on *your* life and the lives of *those you love and lead*. In contrast, ask yourself once again:

- *What could my life look like by taking daily action in the areas I have identified throughout this book?*
- *What positive impact would confronting my limiting beliefs, living with discipline, and pursuing growth have on my leadership and family?*

Leading with excellence is more than operational logistics and organizational management. Leading with excellence is about *leading*

CHAPTER TEN

Dare to Climb

THE "UNCHARTED" FRAMEWORK
9 KEYS FOR PURSUING YOUR POTENTIAL IN LEADERSHIP AND LIFE

U	UNDERSTAND YOUR LIMITING BELIEFS
N	NAVIGATE WITH VISION AND PURPOSE
C	CHOOSE TO TAKE OWNERSHIP
H	HARNESS RESILIENCE
A	ACT WITH DISCIPLINE AND CONSISTENCY
R	REFRAME YOUR MINDSET
T	TRANSFORM FAILURE INTO OPPORTUNITIES
E	EMBRACE COMMUNITY AND ACCOUNTABILITY
D	DARE TO CLIMB

THE GROWTH-MINDED LEADER

There is no easy path up the mountain. As you stand at its base, the only path toward your growth requires something different from you, found only in the things you would likely rather avoid. Your progress up the incline and the mile markers you pass only occur through the ownership you take, the discipline you embody, the resilience you develop, and the failures you learn from. In this place, you will be refined with the character and mindset necessary to take your land and stake your claim on the mountains in your way.

As you near the end of this book, you have two options: You can choose the *discomfort of growth now* to have the life, marriage, relationships, and leadership that you want later, or you can choose *comfort now* and stay stuck in the same place, circling the same mountain over and over again. Reflect back to chapter three on vision and purpose, and ask yourself these questions once more:

- *What would be the cost of inaction in my life one year from now? Three years from now?*
- *What will be the cost of inaction regarding my relationships, health, or impact on my family?*

These are very real questions with very real ramifications on *your* life and the lives of *those you love and lead*. In contrast, ask yourself once again:

- *What could my life look like by taking daily action in the areas I have identified throughout this book?*
- *What positive impact would confronting my limiting beliefs, living with discipline, and pursuing growth have on my leadership and family?*

Leading with excellence is more than operational logistics and organizational management. Leading with excellence is about *leading yourself first*, and then allowing that overflow to add value to every relationship and responsibility entrusted to you. It's about being faithful with what is in your hands. The calling on your life is far bigger than you realize, and your untapped potential is more vast than you can imagine. But the daily question that needs answering is:

Am I willing to show up today and pursue it?

Leave it All on the Field

As a college athlete, I understood the value of the preparation and hard work required to compete at a high level. While playing soccer for Houghton University in western New York, I remember huddling on the windy field before games, arms draped over my teammates' shoulders. As my coach scanned the circle and locked eyes with each of us before the whistle blew, he would say, "Leave everything you have out on the field. Leave nothing left in you when that final whistle blows. You are men with a purpose, so let nothing stop you from achieving it." Those words still resonate with me twenty years later but in a much more meaningful way.

While no other team is competing against you in life, you are still competing—and the competition is *you*. It's found in the moments when the snooze button on your alarm clock seems more enticing than getting up to journal and exercise before your day. It's the moments when it would feel easier to avoid your emotions rather than process them so that you can show up emotionally healthy and regulated for your spouse and children. It's the moments when it would be easier to blame your circumstances rather than take ownership of your perspective and decisions amid them.

As you finish this book, you determine what you will do with the information you have and how you will steward it today, tomorrow, and the next. Les Brown, speaker and author of *Live Your Dreams* (Brown,

2001), shared about the wealthiest place on earth—the graveyard. He writes:

> *The graveyard is the richest place on earth because it is here that you will find all the hopes and dreams that were never fulfilled, the books that were never written, the songs that were never sung, the inventions that were never shared, the cures that were never discovered, all because someone was too afraid to take that first step, keep with the problem, or determined to carry out their dream.*

What is the vision that burns inside you? What imprint do you want to leave on the lives of those you lead? What is the legacy that you want to leave for your family and for your children's children? Every day that you are given is a gift. Take no sunrise for granted, and refuse to let yourself go through the motions. More people count on you than you realize. Your future self counts on you.

The Power of Showing Up

There is an 80% rule for just about anything in life, from real estate to finances to decision-making. When it comes to the 80% rule and the process of your growth, the secret is in consistency:

- 10% of days, you will feel great. You will feel motivated and eager to pursue your vision.
- 10% of days, you will feel terrible. You will feel tired and discouraged and would instead opt for comfort.
- However, your growth and success are ultimately determined by how you show up on the 80% of the days in between.

How you show up on an average day will stack up over time and compound into exponential growth in the long run. The key is having more days of pursuing growth than days settling in your comfort zone. Ask yourself today:

> *If I repeated this day for ninety days, would I be closer to or further from my potential?*

The answer is the information necessary to make the adjustments for tomorrow. If the answer is *further*, beating yourself up about it or partnering with shame will serve you in no way. Instead, recalibrate and wake up tomorrow with intentionality, vision, and action.

You have 1,440 minutes each day. If you take twenty minutes daily to focus on your habits for growth in a specific area, that is less than 2% of your waking hours. However, imagine your connection with your spouse, your relationship with your children, your emotional health, or even your mindset if you committed to it consistently for the next ninety days. There would be recognizable fruit in these areas and momentum to build on. So, what are you waiting for?

> If I repeated this day for 90 days, would I be *closer to* or *further from* my potential?

Choose Your Hard

The life, leadership, and relationships you desire are not waiting for you in the easy things. They are waiting to be discovered on the mountain. When you lean into your challenging times with the proper perspective, you not only emerge on the other side but you are also equipped with the tools necessary to climb the next one. Every season of your life serves a purpose, and it is up to you to find it. Keith Craft, pastor and author of *Your Divine Fingerprint* (Craft, 2013), shared a profound poem in 2019 at a men's conference titled *Choose Your Hard*:

Being your best is hard.
Being normal is hard.
Making wise decisions is hard.
Making bad decisions is hard.
Being in shape is hard.
Being out of shape is hard.
Losing weight is hard.
Being fat is hard.
Working out is hard.
Being weak is hard.
Being disciplined is hard.
Being lazy is hard.
Getting out of your comfort zone is hard.
Staying in your comfort zone is hard.
Starting a business is hard.
Working for someone else is hard.
Making a lot of money is hard.
Making a little bit of money is hard.
Being rich is hard.
Being poor is hard.
Having great relationships is hard.
Having bad relationships is hard.
Having friends is hard.
Having no friends is hard.
Fighting for your marriage is hard.
Divorce is hard.
Having a lot of things is hard.
Having nothing is hard.
Living on purpose is hard.
Living off purpose is hard.
Doing life God's way is hard.
Doing life your own way is hard.

Everything is hard!
Choose your hard!
(Craft, 2022).

This perspective from Craft is a straightforward reminder that nothing worth having of value comes without hard work. On the flip side, the pain of complacency, apathy, and avoidance is a much steeper cost to your life and those around you—one that you cannot afford to pay if you want to live at your fullest potential.

UNCHARTED

The foundation of this book was built on the UNCHARTED Framework, which serves as a roadmap for growth in every area of your life. However, your growth is a choice. So start today, build on it tomorrow, and begin truly *leading your life* rather than simply being *led by it.*

You have incredible potential inside of you, and my prayer for you is that you will embrace the process of growth in your life by confronting your limiting beliefs, staying true to your vision and purpose, taking ownership of your circumstances, persevering with resilience in your trials, living with daily discipline, refining your mindset, embracing setbacks as opportunities, and inviting others to speak into your life.

There are mountains in front of you for the taking. These mountains are not there to stop you; they are intended to strengthen and develop you into the person and leader you are made to be. The question is—will you dare to make the climb?

Epilogue

Throughout this book, I've emphasized the importance of grit, mindset, intentionality, and personal responsibility. I've encouraged you to look within—to confront fear, develop discipline, and choose the path of growth even when it's hard. And while I believe all of that is true and necessary, it's not the whole story.

The deeper truth is this: we were never meant to walk this journey alone or rely solely on our own strength.

My faith in Jesus Christ is the foundation of my life. I know I cannot become the man, husband, father, or leader I desire to be without Him. Everything I've shared in this book is ultimately rooted in that belief. Willpower may carry us part of the way—but true growth and lasting transformation only come through God's grace.

Faith doesn't mean life will be without struggles. In fact, God never promised us an easy life. But He *did* promise His presence and strength in the midst of it. The Bible reminds us over and over that while the journey is hard, we will grow as we lean on Him, renew our minds, and see our situations through the lens of His truth.

Romans 5:3–5 reminds us:

We rejoice in our sufferings, knowing that suffering produces endurance, and endurance produces character, and character produces hope... because God's love has been poured into our hearts through the Holy Spirit. (NIV)

James 1:2–4 also encourages:

Consider it a sheer gift, friends, when tests and challenges come at you from all sides... Don't try to get out of anything prematurely. Let it do its work so you become mature and well-developed, not deficient in any way. (MSG)

That line—*Don't try to get out of anything prematurely*—has always stuck with me. Because it's so easy to escape situations, avoid conversations, and take the easy way out. Doing that may work for a while, but our maturity and growth ultimately depend on the time we spend allowing our trials to refine us.

So yes—do the hard things. Build the discipline. Take ownership of your life. But know this: you don't have to do it alone. God's love, strength, and grace are available to you. You don't have to earn it. And you don't have to "will" your way over the mountains in your life.

If this book has challenged you, encouraged you, or stirred something deeper in you, I hope you'll consider what it means to walk not just *toward* growth—but *with* the One who's with you every step of the way.

The mountains ahead may be steep—but you don't have to climb alone.

References

American Psychological Association. (2018, April 19). *APA dictionary of psychology*. American Psychological Association. https://dictionary.apa.org/resilience

American Psychological Association. (2012). What you need to know about willpower: the psychological science of self-control. American Psychological Association. https://www.apa.org/topics/personality/willpower

Aurelius, M. (2019). *Meditations*. Penguin. (Original work published 180 C.E.)

Bloom, S. (2024, October). 11 things I quit to transform my life. *The Curiosity Chronicle* [Newsletter]. https://www.sahilbloom.com/newsletter/11-things-i-quit-to-transform-my-life

Bloom, S. (2025, January 14). A monthly ritual that changed my life. The Curiosity Chronicle. https://www.sahilbloom.com/newsletter/a-monthly-ritual-that-changed-my-life

Brady, T. [@10xgrowthconference]. (2024, June 17). *Life is not about what happens when you succeed, it's about what happens when you fail.* [Video File]. Retrieved from https://www.instagram.com/p/C8UjaO9gmhw/

Brown, L. (2001). *Live your dreams*. Quill.

Bryksina, O. (2024). When facilitating a group member's (versus one's own) progress increases motivation in group-level goal pursuit. American Psychological Association. https://psycnet.apa.org/fulltext/2024-99484-001.html

Bühler, J. L., Krauss, S., & Orth, U. (2021). Development of relationship satisfaction across the life span: A systematic review and meta-analysis. *Psychological Bulletin, 147*(10), 1012–1053.

Celestine, N. (2015, November 24). How to change limiting beliefs according to psychology. Positive Psychology. https://positivepsychology.com/false-beliefs/

Clary, S. D. (2025, February 5). Stop chasing your dream life… build your perfect day instead. [Article]. LinkedIn. https://www.linkedin.com/pulse/stop-chasing-your-dream-life-build-perfect-day-instead-scott-d-clary-m7dgf/

Claytor, K. [@kenclaytor]. (2024, May 8). *Normalize difficulties.* [Video File]. Retrieved from https://www.instagram.com/kenclaytor/reel/C6uLAwYx9To/

Clear, J. (2018). *Atomic habits: An easy and proven way to build good habits and break bad ones.* Penguin Publishing Group.

Clemmer, J. (2014, July 3). Learned helplessness: The pike syndrome. The Clemer Group. https://www.clemmergroup.com/blog/2014/07/03/canadian-and-american-independence-busting-barriers/

Collins, J. (2001). *Good to great.* Random House.

Connection Codes (n.d.). *Core emotion wheel.* https://www.connectioncodes.co/wheel

Connors, R., Smith, T., & Hickman, C. W. (2014). *The Oz principle: Getting results through individual and organizational accountability.* Penguin Random House.

Cook, T. & Nesloney, T. (2023). *Building authenticity: A blueprint for the leader inside you.* ConnectEDD.

Craft, K. (2022, May 12). Choose your hard. [Video]. Facebook. https://www.facebook.com/watch/?v=342937661265371

Craft, K. (2013). *Your divine fingerprint.* Harper Collins.

Cury, F., Elliot, J., Da Fonseca, D., & Moller, A. (2006). The social-cognitive model of achievement motivation and the 2x2 achievement goal framework. Journal of Personality and Social Psychology, 90(4), 666-679.

David, S. (2022, April 13). Discomfort is the price of admission to a meaningful life. (Host: R. Roll). In *The Rich Roll Podcast.* https://www.susandavid.com/podcast/discomfort-is-the-price-of-admission-to-a-meaningful-life/?trk=public_post_comment-text

REFERENCES

Duckworth, A. (2016). *Grit: The power of passion and perseverance.* Scribner.

Duckworth, A. L., & Seligman, M. E. P. (2005). Self-discipline outdoes IQ in predicting academic performance of adolescents. *Psychological Science, 16*(12), 939-944.

Duke Women's Basketball. (2022, July 5). *Kara Lawson: Handle hard better.* [Video]. Youtube. https://www.youtube.com/watch?v=oDzfZOfNki4

Dweck, C. (2017). *Mindset: Changing the way you think to fulfill your potential.* Robinson.

Dweck, C. (1999). Self-theories: Their role in motivation, personality, and development. Psychology Press.

Dykes, D.O. (2017, November 16). Faith to endure tough times. David O. Dykes Sermon Archive. https://gabc-archive.org/wp-content/uploads/2018/12/s112617.pdf

Gallup. (2024). *State of the global workplace report.* Gallup. https://www.gallup.com/workplace/349484/state-of-the-global-workplace.aspx

Gardner, W.L., Avolio, B.J., Luthans, F., May, D.R., Walumbwa, F. (2005). "Can you see the real me?" A self-based model of authentic leader and follower development. The Leadership Quarterly, 16(3), 343-372.

George, W., Sims, P., McLean, A.N., Mayer, D. (2007). Discovering your authentic leadership. Harvard Business Review, 1-8.

Gibson, M. (Director). (1995). Braveheart [Film]. Paramount Pictures.

Gladwell, M. (2008). *Outliers: The story of success.* Back Bay Books.

Goggins, D. (2018). *Can't hurt me: Master your mind and defy the odds.* Lioncrest Publishing.

Goodreads. (n.d.) A quote from André Gide. Retrieved December 14, 2024, from https://www.goodreads.com/author/quotes/7617.Andr_Gide

Goodreads. (n.d.). A quote from Mickey Rooney. Retrieved December 20, 2024, from https://www.goodreads.com/author/quotes/613577.Mickey_Rooney

Gunn, R. J. (2009). *Coming attractions.* Zondervan.

Hanson, R. (2010, October 26). Confronting the negativity bias. Psychology Today. https://www.psychologytoday.com/us/blog/your-wise-brain/201010/confronting-the-negativity-bias

Hayden, J. (2024). Why you should stop complaining today, backed by neuroscience. Inc. https://www.inc.com/jeff-haden/why-you-should-stop-complaining-today-backed-by-neuroscience.html

Heflick, N. (2011, November 23). The spotlight effect: Do as many people notice us as we think? Psychology Today. https://www.psychologytoday.com/us/blog/the-big-questions/201111/the-spotlight-effect

Holiday, R. (2015). *The obstacle is the way: The ancient art of turning adversity to advantage.* Profile Books.

Huberman, A. (2021). The anterior midcingulate cortex and its role in resilience. In *Huberman Lab Podcast: The Science of Stress and How to Manage It.* Episode 34. Huberman Lab.

Hutchinson, J. (2019, July 30). The elephant and the rope: What you believe is powerful! The We Spot. https://thewespot.com/the-elephant-and-the-rope-what-you-believe-is-powerful/

Ionescu, I. (2021, April 6). Benjamin Franklin's 13 life virtues. Thrive Global. https://community.thriveglobal.com/benjamin-franklins-13-life-virtues/

Jackley, J. (2015). *Clay water brick.* Random House.

Jocko Podcast. (2015, December 31). Jocko Podcast #3 - With Echo Charles | "The Last Hundred Yards" Book, Jiu Jitsu, Bosses, Failure. [Video]. Youtube. https://www.youtube.com/watch?v=XdntJrOJ4rs

Kallio, C. (2020, April 7). The cost of inaction. My Working Mind. https://www.workingmymind.com/the-cost-of-inaction-in-life/

Kiva's Impact. (n.d.). Kiva. https://www.kiva.org/impact

Kleck, R. & Strenta, A. (1980). Perceptions of the impact of negatively valued characteristics on social interaction. Journal of Personality and Social Psychology. 39. 861-873.

Klinghoffer, D., & Kirkpatrick-Husk, K. (2023, May 18). *More than 50% of managers feel burned out.* Harvard Business Review. https://hbr.org/2023/05/more-than-50-of-managers-feel-burned-out

Kristensen, S. (2023, April 5). 21 limiting belief examples that are holding you back in life. Happier Human. https://www.happierhuman.com/limiting-beliefs/

REFERENCES

Krockow, E. (2018, September 27). How many decisions do we make each day? Psychology Today. https://www.psychologytoday.com/us/blog/stretching-theory/201809/how-many-decisions-do-we-make-each-day

Leahy, R. L. (2005). *The worry cure: Seven steps to stop worry from stopping you.* Harmony Books.

Magness, S. [@stevemagness]. (2024, December 28). *Want to improve at anything? Show up.* Retrieved from https://www.instagram.com/p/DEH7ofUocb_/?img_index=1

Mandela, N. (2014). *Long walk to freedom.* Macmillan Children's Books.

Marshall, L. (2018, November 14). The more pain you expect, the more you feel, study shows. CU Boulder Today. https://www.colorado.edu/today/2018/11/14/more-pain-you-expect-more-you-feel-new-study-shows

Neal, D. T., Wood, W., & Quinn, J. M. (2006). Habits - A repeated performance. Current Direction in Psychological Science. https://web.archive.org/web/20110526144503/http://dornsife.usc.edu/wendywood/research/documents/Neal.Wood.Quinn.2006.pdf

New International Version Bible. (2011). Bible Gateway. https://biblegateway.com.

No Barriers (n.d.). Founders. https://nobarriersusa.org/about-us/founders/

No Barriers (n.d.). No barriers. https://nobarriersusa.org

Ochoa, E. (n.d.). Ellen Ochoa. https://ellenochoa.com/biography/

Pritchett, P. & Pritchett, P. (1994). *You 2.* Conran Octopus.

Ramis, H. (Director). 1993. Groundhog's Day. Columbia Pictures.

Reynolds, W. A. (1959). The burning ships of Hernán Cortés. *Hispania,* 42(3), 317–324. https://doi.org/10.2307/335707

Rohn, J. (2024). *Take charge of your life.* Sound Wisdom.

Rohn, J. (2018, November 2). The result of your life is determined by a few simple disciplines. Jim Rohn International. https://www.jimrohn.com/a-few-simple-disciplines/

Roosevelt, F. (1938, April 14). Franklin Roosevelt: Fireside Chat. [Radio Broadcast]. https://archive.org/details/firesidechats_1705_librivox

Seek to Do More. (n.d.). Seek to Do More. https://seektodomore.com/

Shadyac, T. (Director). (2007). *Evan Almighty* [Film]. Spyglass Entertainment.

Sinrich, J. (2023, July 24). Stories that prove it's never too late to change in life. Reader's Digest. https://www.rd.com/list/never-too-late-change-your-life/

TED. (2017, February 2). *Extreme Ownership | Jocko Willink*. [Video]. Youtube. https://www.youtube.com/watch?v=ljqra3BcqWM

The Message Bible. (2018). Bible Gateway. https://biblegateway.com.

The Strive. (n.d.). Tom Brady Success Story. The Strive. https://thestrive.co/tom-brady-success-story/

Thomas, D. (2024, November 12). 30 greatest Michael Jordan quotes. Your Positive Oasis. https://yourpositiveoasis.com/30-greatest-michael-jordan-quotes/

Willink, J. & Babin, L. (2015). *Extreme ownership*. Macmillan.

Wood, G. & Hornberger, T. (n.d.). Benjamin Franklin. In Encyclopedia Brittanica. Retrieved December 4, 2024 from https://www.britannica.com/biography/Benjamin-Franklin

Vasari, G. (1991). *Lives of the artists* (G. Bull, Trans.). Penguin Classics. (Original work published 1550).

Viswesvaran, C., Sanchez, J. I., & Fisher, J. (1999). The role of social support in the process of work stress: A meta-analysis. *Journal of Applied Psychology*, 84(2), 311–321.

Ziglar, Inc. (2013, January 8). Zig Ziglar: Attitude makes all the difference. [Video]. Youtube. https://www.youtube.com/watch?v=_bkVZ1kD8Xo

Zint, J. (n.d.). The Habit Lab. https://thehabitlab.org/

About the Author

Dr. Tyler Cook is the principal of Klein Elementary School in the Harbor Creek School District in Erie, Pennsylvania. He is also a keynote speaker, leadership coach, adjunct professor at PennWest University, and co-author of *Building Authenticity: A Blueprint for the Leader Inside You*. He holds a doctorate in Leadership and Administration from Point Park University, where his research focused on authentic leadership development. Tyler is passionate about developing healthy, high-impact leaders who will grow their teams and organizations to their fullest potential. He lives in Erie with his wife, Stacey, and their four children: Elijah, Judah, Noah, and Anna. Connect with Tyler on his website at www.drtylercook.com.

More from ConnectEDD Publishing

Since 2015, ConnectEDD has worked to transform education by empowering educators to become better-equipped to teach, learn, and lead. What started as a small company designed to provide professional learning events for educators has grown to include a variety of services to help educators and administrators address essential challenges. ConnectEDD offers instructional and leadership coaching, professional development workshops focusing on a variety of educational topics, a roster of nationally recognized educator associates who possess hands-on knowledge and experience, educational conferences custom-designed to meet the specific needs of schools, districts, and state/national organizations, and ongoing, personalized support, both virtually and onsite. In 2020, ConnectEDD expanded to include publishing services designed to provide busy educators with books and resources consisting of practical information on a wide variety of teaching, learning, and leadership topics. Please visit us online at connecteddpublishing.com or contact us at: info@connecteddpublishing.com

Recent Publications:

Live Your Excellence: Action Guide by Jimmy Casas

Culturize: Action Guide by Jimmy Casas

Daily Inspiration for Educators: Positive Thoughts for Every Day of the Year by Jimmy Casas

Eyes on Culture: Multiply Excellence in Your School by Emily Paschall

Pause. Breathe. Flourish. Living Your Best Life as an Educator by William D. Parker

L.E.A.R.N.E.R. Finding the True, Good, and Beautiful in Education by Marita Diffenbaugh

Educator Reflection Tips Volume II: Refining Our Practice by Jami Fowler-White

Handle With Care: Managing Difficult Situations in Schools with Dignity and Respect by Jimmy Casas and Joy Kelly

Disruptive Thinking: Preparing Learners for Their Future by Eric Sheninger

Permission to be Great: Increasing Engagement in Your School by Dan Butler

Daily Inspiration for Educators: Positive Thoughts for Every Day of the Year, Volume II by Jimmy Casas

The 6 Literacy Levers: Creating a Community of Readers by Brad Gustafson

The Educator's ATLAS: Your Roadmap to Engagement by Weston Kieschnick

In This Season: Words for the Heart by Todd Nesloney, LaNesha Tabb, Tanner Olson, and Alice Lee

Leading with a Humble Heart: A 40-Day Devotional for Leaders by Zac Bauermaster

Recalibrate the Culture: Our Why…Our Work…Our Values by Jimmy Casas

Creating Curious Classrooms: The Beauty of Questions by Emma Chiappetta

MORE FROM CONNECTEDD PUBLISHING

Crafting the Culture: 45 Reflections on What Matters Most by Joe Sanfelippo and Jeffrey Zoul

Improving School Mental Health: The Thriving School Community Solution by Charle Peck and Dr. Cameron Caswell

Building Authenticity: A Blueprint for the Leader Inside You by Todd Nesloney and Tyler Cook

Connecting Through Conversation: A Playbook for Talking with Kids by Erika Bare and Tiffany Burns

The Dream Factory: Designing a Purposeful Life by Mark Trumbo

Stories Behind Stances: Creating Empathy Through Hearing "The Other Side" by Chris Singleton

Happy Eyes: Becoming All Things to All People by Ryan Tillman

The Generative Age: Artificial Intelligence and the Future of Education by Alana Winnick

Recalibrate the Culture: Action Guide by Jimmy Casas

Leading with PEOPLE: A Six Pillar Framework for Fruitful Leadership by Zac Bauermaster

A School Leader's Guide to Reclaiming Purpose by Frederick C. Buskey

Foundations of an Elite Culture: Building Success with High Standards and a Positive Environment by David Arencibia

Personalize: Meeting the Needs of All Learners by Eric Sheninger and Nicki Slaugh

The Five Principles of Educator Professionalism: Rebuilding Trust in Schools by Nason Lollar

Words on the Wall: Culturizing Your Classroom for Observable Impact by Jimmy Casas and Cale Birk

School of Engagement: 45 Activities to Ignite Student Learning by Jonathan Alsheimer

Intentional Instructional Moves: Strategic Steps to Accelerate Student Learning by Sherry St. Clair

Overcoming Education: Complex Challenges, Difficult People, and the Art of Making a Difference by Brad R. Gustafson

The Language of Behavior: A Framework to Elevate Student Success by Charle Peck and Joshua Stamper

Whose Permission Are You Waiting For? An Educator's Guide to Doing What You Love by William D. Parker

The Leader You're Not…And Why It's Just As Important As the Leader You Are by Scott Borba

www.ingramcontent.com/pod-product-compliance
Lightning Source LLC
Chambersburg PA
CBHW070625030426
42337CB00020B/3918